JACO PASTORIUS
BASS METHOD

PLAYBACK+
Speed · Pitch · Balance · Loop

Lessons, Tips, and Techniques
from His Private Teaching Archives

BY RAY PETERSON

To access audio visit:
www.halleonard.com/mylibrary

Enter Code
5752-9562-9561-6434

Cover Photo © Ebet Roberts

Audio tracks mastered by Michael Dominici, Music House Mastering

ISBN 978-0-634-02031-5

HAL•LEONARD®
CORPORATION
7777 W. BLUEMOUND RD. P.O. BOX 13819 MILWAUKEE, WI 53213

Visit Hal Leonard Online at
www.halleonard.com

Contents

Preface

Perhaps you're standing in a music store right now, reading this introduction and wondering, "What makes this an authentic Jaco Pastorius bass method book? Who the heck wrote this?" Fair enough!

I grew up in Fort Lauderdale, FL as an aspiring bassist with strong jazz and rock leanings. Still in my teens, I had played in rock bands, done some gigging in Miami on the R&B circuit, and begun to delve into serious music studies. I kept hearing about this electric bass player, Jaco Pastorius, who was supposedly tearing it up around town. My girlfriend at the time, Cathy Vieira, worked for a dentist who was also a trombone player. He insisted that I absolutely *had* to come with him to The Lion's Share, a club in nearby Hollywood, to hear the notorious Jaco play with jazz great Ira Sullivan. I figured, sure, this guy's got to be pretty good, right? Let's go!

About eight measures into the first tune, I almost fell to the floor! I had never seen or heard anything like it. This guy in a jersey, pants that were too short, and sneakers was *all over* the bass. He always seemed to know exactly what he was doing and where he was, no matter how far out the music went. The concept of bass playing he displayed struck a youngster like myself as being absolutely revolutionary. It was as if two of my heroes, Scott LaFaro and Jack Bruce, had somehow combined into one monster who was also steeped in Latin music and funk. I felt inspired as never before to practice my instrument assiduously.

Some months later, Cathy called me at home to ask me, "Guess who's coming in to have his kid's teeth worked on? Jaco!" My reply was simple: "I'll be right there!"

I drove down to the dentist's office and introduced myself while Jaco was standing in the hallway waiting for his kids. We talked about music for awhile, and I asked him if he did any teaching. He seemed rather disinterested in teaching me, but I gave him my number anyway, just in case. Incidentally, our dentist friend persuaded him to get in the chair for a quick checkup before leaving. In typical Jaco fashion, he replied, "I've never had a cavity in my life." The good doctor's brief examination revealed this to be absolutely true. This was my introduction to the reality that Jaco could invariably back up his seemingly ridiculous claims with cold hard facts.

Some weeks later, I came home one evening and was informed by my brother Ronnie that Jaco had called. Talk about excitement! When I called him back, he informed me that he had heard good things about me and wondered if I still wanted to take lessons. That would be a no-brainer, folks.

So it came to pass that I became Jaco's student, assimilating his brilliant common-sense perspectives on music and the bass guitar (and life) for more than a decade.

A few days after the call, I drove up to his house for the first lesson and knocked on the door. No answer. No car out front. After a short wait, Jaco came driving up with his family. He emerged from the car in shorts, no shirt, and a wooden paddle in hand. "Sorry I'm late," he offered. "I was playing in a paddleball tournament."

Inside the house, I saw the list of tunes for his as-of-yet unrecorded first album taped to the wall. He had a few boxes of records on the floor, which we looked through for a few minutes. He held up albums by Clarence Carter ("This guy has more soul than ten cats!"), Jimi Hendrix, Paul Hindemith, Bill Evans, Maceo Parker, Edgar Winter's White Trash—now, here was a guy with taste.

Thus began a journey into a world of brilliant common-sense solutions to vexing musical problems spawned from the mind of the inimitable Mr. Pastorius. He had the most remarkable way of breaking down music theory and stating it in a way that anyone could understand and apply practically (knowledge that conventional music educators love to present in the most pedantic terms). He loved to cut through pretense and get right to the core of the musical matter in a logical and concise fashion. Jaco represented a combination of unpretentious earthiness, razor-sharp musical intelligence, and erudition. His approach to theory has shaped my own conception to this day.

Over the years, we became good friends as well, frequently attending each other's gigs. Jaco was a huge fan of the band I played in, fronted by steel drum master Othello Molineaux, and would often sit in at our shows. He would regularly refer bassists who asked him for lessons to me ("They're getting the same lesson"), as he was touring too much to take on students. He even played one of my compositions, "Leapfrog," with his Word of Mouth Band. Jaco also called me to play bass at the initial rehearsal for "Liberty City" while he conducted Peter Graves's big band (with Peter Erskine on drums—are we having fun yet?). On a couple of occasions, he called me on stage where he was performing, handed me his bass... and *left the stage*, most memorably on my very first night in New York (where I've lived for more than 20 years) at the old Lone Star Cafe. He was always looking for ways to freak people out (a.k.a. "the total wipe"), and I know on these occasions he definitely succeeded in the case of your humble author.

Over the course of this volume, it is my hope to provide the student with the same knowledge that I received from the master. In short, if the student wishes he could have studied with Jaco, I hope to take him as close as realistically possible to that goal, while humbly realizing the obvious impossibility of this task. Having been asked to pen this method book, I feel duty-bound to share the wealth of valuable information he gave me with the rest of the bass-playing world.

As Jaco was fond of pointing out, "The only shortcut is the long way," and "Don't wait for some cat to tell you that you have the ability." In that spirit, let's dive in!

Using This Book

This book offers the possibility of multiple approaches. While aimed at the intermediate player who wishes to advance, there is plenty of material for the advanced player in the later sections of the book. If you are an advanced player and feel you have already mastered scales and chords, feel free to tackle the melodic exercises and solo transcriptions straight away. If you have not yet mastered these technical hurdles, I suggest you do so, at least to some degree, before tackling the more complicated material. I also recommend practicing chords and the scales that fit over them together in addition to practicing scales or chords separately. For example, practice the Dorian mode immediately after practicing minor seventh chords, etc. Do not feel confined to going through this book one page at a time. However, if you find yourself absolutely baffled by any of the advanced content, it's a sure sign that you need to reinforce the basics. Don't get too far ahead of yourself.

Although tablature has been provided (reading music is not necessarily a prerequisite of using this book), I should point out that Jaco was big on the idea of sightreading. Whenever anyone asked him about studying, reading was invariably one of the first subjects he would bring up. If you cannot read music, I strongly urge you to pick up a basic reading method and get started. Granted, reading is not essential to many playing situations. Record stores and music magazines are chock-full of examples of successful artists who can't read music. Having said that, if you want to play jazz or classical music, become a studio player, or decipher music as complex as that of Jaco Pastorius, reading is a skill you can ill afford to overlook. Your purchase of this book proves that you are interested in the pursuit of excellence. Follow through on that instinct and get your reading together if you haven't already done so.

I also highly recommend that you acquire a keyboard and begin studying harmony in addition to practicing your bass. It is vitally important to understand how chords work and to hear them played on the piano. The chord examples in the harmonic section of the book, in particular, will make much more sense if you actually play the chords.

1. Basic Technique

"Make every note count."

One of the things Jaco said to me during that first phone call was that his teaching method was about "really building cats' hands up." Needless to say, this turned out to be exactly the case. Building a strong set of bass hands requires developing good habits, so let's discuss the basics of technique.

Left Hand

Keep the fingers of your left hand curved. Don't allow the knuckles to cave in. If you let the knuckles collapse, you will weaken the force being brought down on the string, leading to a less-articulated tone. A span of three frets (for example, third to fifth fret) should be played with the first finger on the lower note and the fourth finger on the upper note. The second and third fingers should remain on the string behind the fourth finger when playing the upper note. When playing with this correct hand-positioning, the hand should resemble a claw. A span of five frets (for example, third fret to seventh fret) should be played in a similar fashion with the fourth finger stretching to the top note. The second finger should be used to play the note halfway between (the fifth fret, in this case). You should work to build this stretch early on. One of the best examples of this is found in the whole-tone scale:

Another fingering technique I learned from Jaco involves sliding the first finger one fret (half step) when you need to extend your fingering in a passage. A prime example of this is the diminished scale:

Keep the thumb behind the neck of the bass. Letting the thumb hook over the neck will lead to weak technique. I thoughtlessly did this once while asking Jaco a question. He looked at my hands and said, "First get your thumb behind the neck where it belongs." That should give you an idea of the importance he placed on this issue. Most bass players I see let their thumb hook over the top. Do so at your own peril!

Right Hand

Jaco, of course, played fingerstyle, so that is the right-hand style we will discuss. Pick with the first two fingers of your right hand, keeping the fingers slightly curved. Don't let the knuckle nearest the tip of the finger collapse when you pluck the string. The effect should be more of pulling the finger back over the string, rather than slapping down on it with the fingers.

I once asked him about thumb placement (at that time, I tended to anchor my thumb on the bridge pickup). He answered that, "It just hangs out around the E string." Over time, I adopted that technique myself, especially when playing the 5- and 6-string bass. This gives the right hand a looser, mobile feeling.

In Jaco's punchy, staccato style, the right hand plays over the bridge pickup. There are two factors that give this position more speed and bite in your playing: One is the increased string tension of this position, which gives the notes a sharper, more focused attack. The other is the closeness of the pickup, which allows the fingers to bounce off it, rather than fall between the strings after hitting the note. I generally like to raise the back pickup as high as possible without the string hitting it on impact.

Jaco's sustained, legato style requires picking closer to the neck. The lessened tension of the strings at this position creates more sustain, giving that "singing" tone. Different points on the string will give you different variations in tone, so experiment with different areas. This position is also preferred for playing walking bass lines.

The Sound

In addition to the magic residing in his hands, the basic steps in getting the "Jaco sound" are:

1. Get a pre-CBS Fender Jazz Bass. (His Fender signature is a faithful replication, or one of the fine Fender vintage replicas.)

2. String it up with Rotosound Swing Bass strings.

3. Turn the neck pickup off. (Personally, I like a little bit on, but this is Jaco's style.)

4. Turn the bridge pickup all the way up.

5. Control the volume from your amp.

The Fretless Bass

Truthfully, our lessons were always done on fretted basses. Fretless playing was not a common topic in the lessons, but Jaco did point out to me once that it was important to hit the note first, and then execute the vibrato, as opposed to playing the vibrato immediately. I believe my first time playing a fretless bass was when he brought his fretless down to an Othello gig and let me try it out. After noting the look of bewilderment on my face, he pointed out that you have to play right where the fret would be in order to play in tune.

2. Basic Theory

In the Western tonal system, the *octave* (distance between a note and the next higher or lower note of the same pitch) is divided into twelve half steps. A *half step* is the span from one fret to the next on any one string or one key to the next on a piano. All twelve half steps in an octave played successively make up the *chromatic scale*.

Two successive half steps combine to form a *whole step*. Different combinations of half and whole steps form various types of scales and chords. A major scale, for example, is a combination of two units consisting of whole step–whole step–half step (shown below as W–W–H), each lying a whole step apart from one another. Each of these two units is called a *tetrachord*. This is demonstrated here with a C major scale.

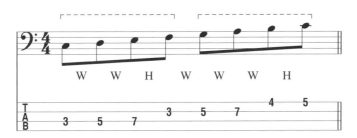

The distance between any two notes is called an *interval*. The following chart shows the intervals available within an octave starting from C:

Interval	Pitch of Interval
Minor 2nd	D♭
Major 2nd	D
Minor 3rd	E♭
Major 3rd	E
Perfect 4th	F
Augmented 4th (Diminished 5th)	F♯ (G♭)
Perfect 5th	G
Minor 6th (Augmented 5th)	A♭ (G♯)
Major 6th	A
Minor 7th	B♭
Major 7th	B
Octave	C

Learn to associate the interval with both its sound in your ears (and head) and shape on the neck when you play it. I always like to use riffs or songs that I know well to conjure up the sound of an interval in my head. For example, the beginning of "Proud Mary" is a downward minor 3rd. The main riff in "Black Sabbath" is an octave up followed by a ♭5th down. Use whatever musical association works best for you.

Two of the most fundamental intervallic building blocks, harmonically speaking, are 5ths and 3rds. We will cover 3rds more extensively in the chapter on "Harmonic Elements." For now, we will focus on 5ths and an important set of key relationships in music called the *Circle of Fifths*:

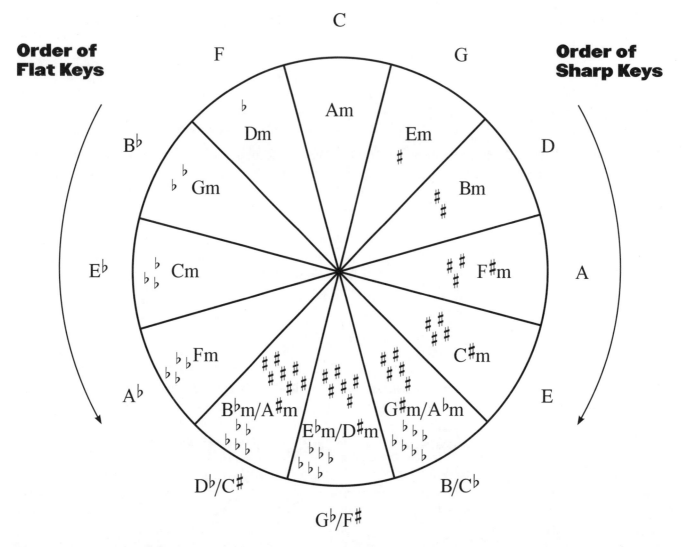

The type of harmonic motion you will encounter in jazz standards is commonly based on this sequence. Moving down in perfect 5ths from C (counterclockwise from 12:00) gives us C–F–B♭–E♭–A♭–D♭–F♯–B–E–A–D–G–C. As we progress through this cycle, we add one flat to each new key, starting with the key of F (one flat, B♭). Each added flat in each new key is, in turn, a 5th down (or 4th up) from the previously added flat. Therefore, the next key in the cycle, B♭, would contain two flats, B♭ and E♭, etc. When we arrive at the key of G♭ at the 6:00 position (which can also be spelled as F♯), we start to consider the remaining keys to be "sharp" keys. F♯ contains six sharps (F♯–C♯–G♯–D♯–A♯–E♯). We subtract one sharp from each of the following keys until we arrive back at C. You can also start at 12:00 (C) and move clockwise (up a 5th) through the sharp keys, adding a sharp to each new key. Hence, the first sharp key (G) contains one sharp, F♯. The second key (D) contains two sharps, F♯ and C♯, etc. Memorize this sequence, along with how many flats or sharps are in each key, and always practice *every* scale and chord you learn in all the keys along the sequence. This is crucial to developing your skills as a musician and will make matters like harmony, scales, intervals, and key changes much simpler for you.

3. Harmonic Elements

"Human beings have nothing to do with music. Music is in the air; you just have to pull it out."

One characteristic that truly sets Jaco apart from the rest of the bass world, particularly at the time of his arrival on the scene, is the breadth and scope of his harmonic knowledge and vision. In my lessons with him, it seemed that we were always analyzing every exercise or piece of music in terms of how the individual bass notes and phrases related to the harmonic content. He once told me that wherever he went in his travels, people tended to remark that he "always played harmonic solos." He answered them to the effect that anyone can play "outside" and that playing harmonically necessitates knowing what you're doing. Indeed, analyses of his solos reveal these ideas time and time again—"inside" statement of the harmony, expansion into chromatic passages, followed by a return to the harmony. This approach requires complete mastery of the harmonic material.

Jaco was a great lover of J.S. Bach, Igor Stravinsky, Paul Hindemith (he claimed to have "almost memorized" Hindemith's Op. 50, *Concert Music for Strings and Brass*), and Charles Ives. I can remember sitting at his grand piano one time as we examined the score to Ives's *Three Places in New England (Orchestra Set No. 1)*. Jaco correctly pointed out that many of the harmonic devices associated with jazz were actually developed decades (or more) earlier by classical composers. In fact, if I had to pick the most important and most emphasized part of my studies with Jaco, it would undoubtedly be the classical literature we covered. In particular, we focused on Justus Friedrich Dotzauer's *113 Studies for Cello Solo* and Bach's *Two-Part Inventions, Six Suites for Cello Solo*, and later, *Chromatic Fantasy*. I can't highly recommend these volumes enough for expanding your technique over the length of the instrument, as well as enriching your musical ear harmonically and melodically. The student would do well not to overlook these books.

Jaco once stated very pointedly, as I opened a Bach exercise on the music stand, that practicing this material was important because "this is pure music." Two of the most frequent expressions I heard him use were "legit" and "jive." He liked to look at music in one of these two ways. I suggest you approach these works in like fashion, realizing the legitimacy and purity of their musical value. Jaco would analyze a classical work like a *Two-Part Invention* the same way he'd analyze a jazz solo, using jazz chord nomenclature (Dm7), rather than the classical analysis using Roman numerals (ii7). He encouraged me to approach my classical exercises the same way. Once you have the etudes under your hands, you, as a student, should do likewise.

From a harmonic standpoint, he absolutely loved the music of Herbie Hancock—particularly the *Speak Like a Child* and *The Prisoner* albums. This harmonic approach is also heard on another one of Jaco's favorites, Gershwin's *Porgy and Bess*, as performed by Miles Davis (featuring the orchestrations of Gil Evans), as well as the work of pianist Bill Evans. These artists were all hugely influential on Jaco's harmonic craft.

We will begin with simple triad structures, moving on to seventh chords with their harmonic extensions. We will conclude this section with a brief discussion of harmonics, including a transcription of his harmonics masterpiece, "Portrait of Tracy."

Triads

Triads are the basic building blocks of harmony in Western music. Even the most complex chord structure we encounter in modern jazz can be broken down into triads ("unless it's just totally out," as I recall Jaco putting it). There are four types of triads:

1. *Major* (major 3rd and minor 3rd)

2. *Minor* (minor 3rd and major 3rd)

3. *Augmented* (major 3rd and major 3rd)

4. *Diminished* (minor 3rd and minor 3rd)

I have grouped the triads in these keys to illustrate some basic principles. A minor is the *relative minor* of C major. Both keys contain the same notes. The relative minor of any major key lies a major 6th up (or minor 3rd down) from the tonic of that key. Playing the relative minor over a major chord yields a very open sound. This is an approach favored by country and blues players.

We refer to the bottom note as the *root* of the chord, the middle note as the 3rd of the chord, and the top note as the 5th of the chord. The augmented triad can also be thought of as a major triad with a ♯5th. A diminished triad can be looked at as a minor triad with a ♭5th.

It is essential to learn to play, hear, and spell all triads in all keys. If you have a solid foundation with all triads, it will make it that much easier for you when you start to tackle more complicated harmonic structures. Further, without a thorough knowledge of triads, understanding more complex harmony becomes impossible. We'll start with the basic structures, later moving on to the diatonic triads found within the major scale. These will facilitate opening up the fingerboard to you as well. I encourage you to master these pages thoroughly before moving on. Avoid merely playing the notes mechanically; spell each chord mentally as you play the exercise. It's also a good idea to spell chords in your head while you're in line at the bank, watching television, or waiting for a train. You'll be amazed at how quickly this helps create a "musical computer" in your brain. Jaco once told me after we played one of his original exercises, "My mind is like a computer, constantly thinking up this sick stuff." Never underestimate the power of mental practice.

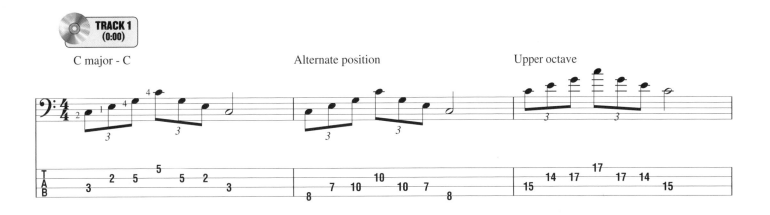

TRACK 1 (0:00)

C major - C   Alternate position   Upper octave

Two octaves

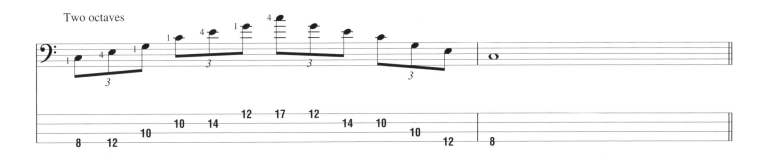

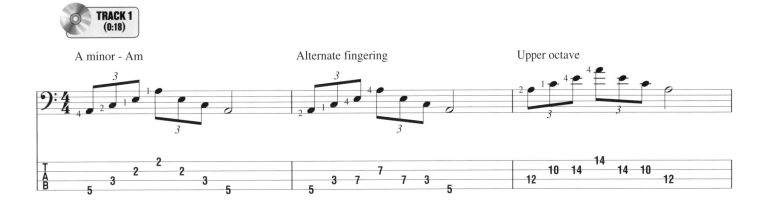

TRACK 1 (0:18)

A minor - Am   Alternate fingering   Upper octave

Two octaves

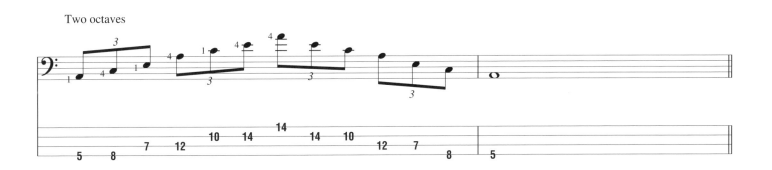

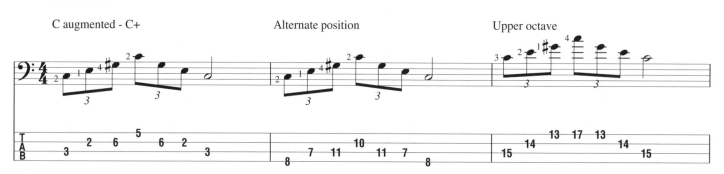

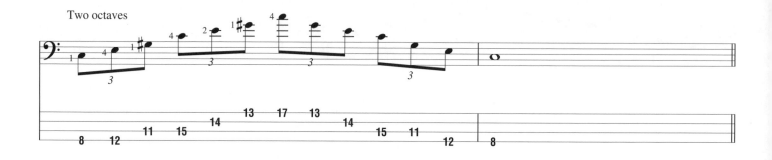

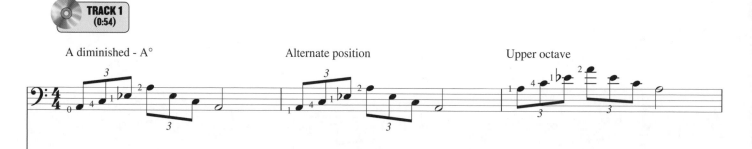

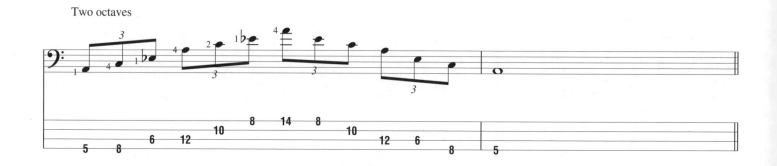

Diatonic Triads

We can take each degree of the major scale and build triads going up the scale diatonically. If the triads are played with the root of the chords on the bottom, this is called *root position*:

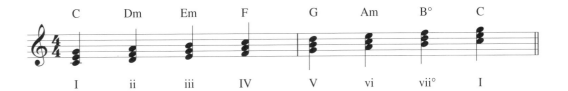

If the triads are played with the 3rd of each chord on the bottom, this is called *first inversion*:

If triads are played with the 5th of the chord on the bottom, they are said to be in *second inversion*:

The I, IV, and V triads are major; the ii, iii, and vi triads are minor; and the vii triad is diminished.

In the following exercises, we will change the top two notes of both first and second inversions in order to spread them out on the fingerboard better. These exercises will build your hands in addition to training your brain and ear. They sound really cool on the bass, as well. In addition to playing them as arpeggios, you should practice playing them as blocked chords, using the thumb and first two fingers to pluck the notes of the chords simultaneously. Make sure you have all three of these exercises down pat before going on to the next one.

Since these exercises cover an entire octave going up and down the neck, playing them in some keys will necessitate playing part of the exercise in a lower register. The most musical and logical way to do this is to change registers at the start of a new tetrachord. Hence, I have written these examples in C and in F, as this will illustrate the shifts you will need to apply to any key.

Root Position Triads

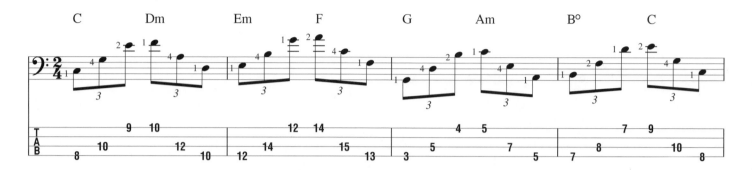

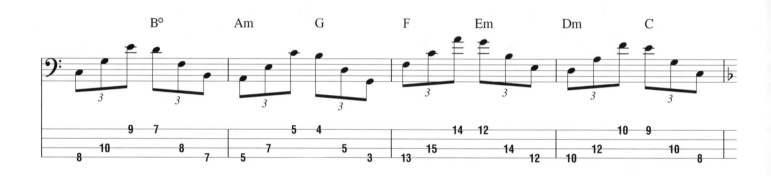

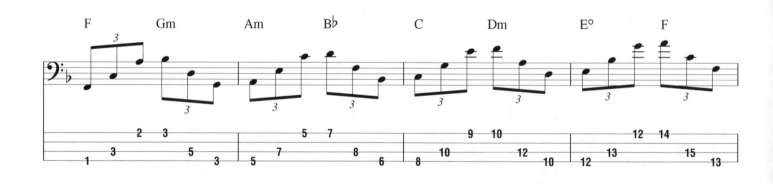

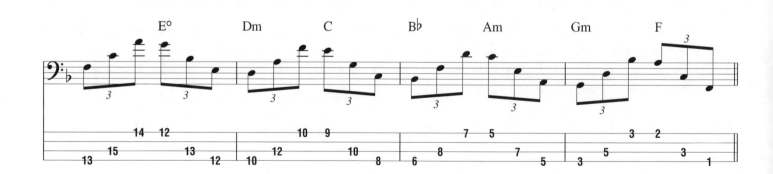

First Inversion Triads

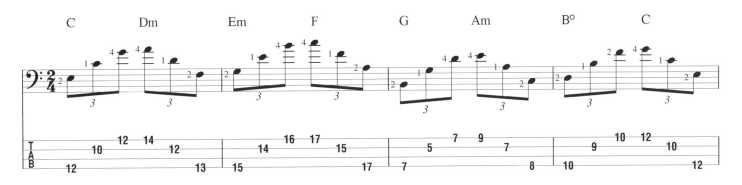

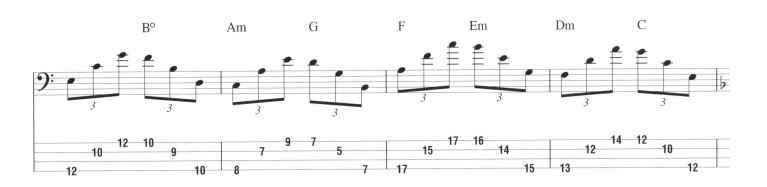

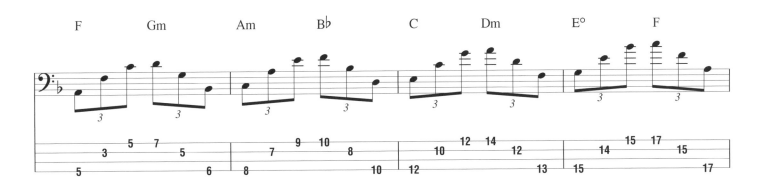

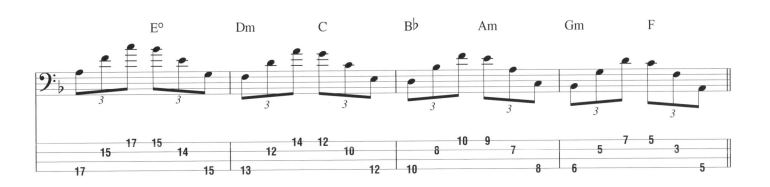

Second Inversion Triads

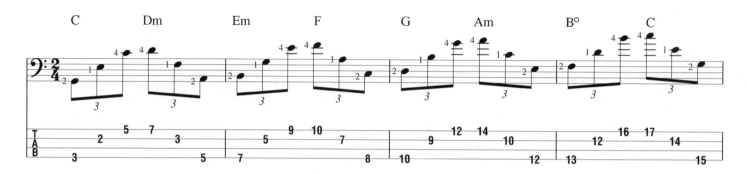

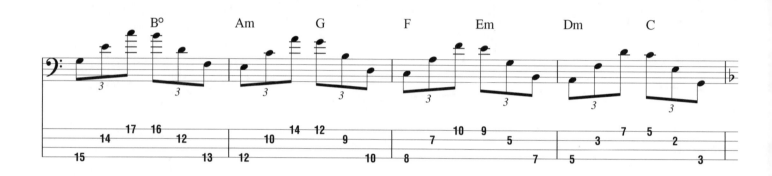

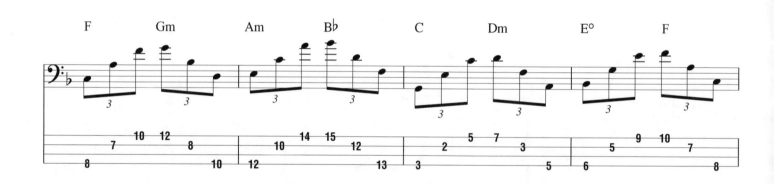

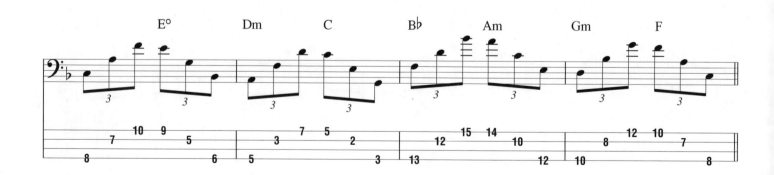

Alternating Diatonic Triads with Tritone Relationships

Let's make things a little more interesting with an exercise Jaco taught me. We'll take the second inversion triads we just learned and alternate them with the corresponding root position triad a tritone (♭5 interval) away. To summarize, in Exercise I, play the second inversion triad going up, followed by the root position triad (a tritone away) coming down. Exercise II is simply a reversal of this—i.e., root position going up, second inversion coming down. In addition to the technical stretching you'll gain from this exercise, you'll also expand your ear's ability to hear the more "outside" extensions of a given tonality. It's also great for training your brain in thinking about *flat five substitutions*. Substituting a seventh chord with another seventh chord a tritone away is a commonly used technique in jazz. For now, let's look at the tritone relationship between two triads:

The tritone divides the octave in half. The melodic tension created by this interval gives us the basic flavor for the much-loved dominant seventh jazz voicings. For example, in the figure above, the chord a tritone up from C is spelled two ways: as G♭ or F♯. If we were to superimpose the G♭ triad over C, it would give us the ♭5th (G♭), ♭7th (B♭), and ♭9th (D♭). Later, we will see how extending triads creates common tones that can be used to exploit the tritone relationship. Mastering the next two exercises will give you a solid foundation for approaching flat five substitutions. I also highly recommend playing these chords on a piano if possible, and, as always, practice in all keys, paying attention to the chords you are playing. Again, don't just play the notes; be aware that you are building up your "mental library." Be conscious of the changes. This was a prime point of Jaco's teaching. If you drill these into your head while practicing, you'll make this information more subconscious, thus freeing your mind to play.

Exercise I

TRACK 5

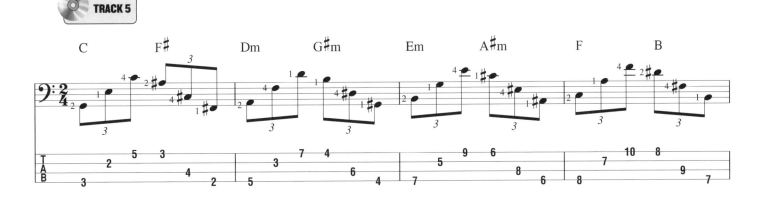

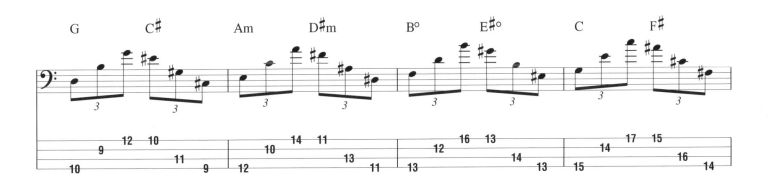

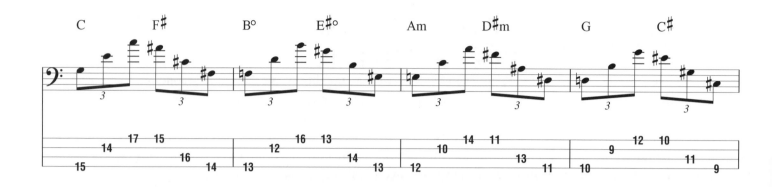

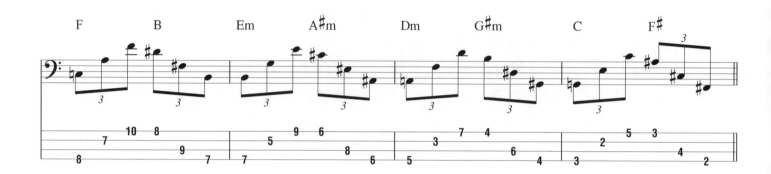

Exercise II

TRACK 6

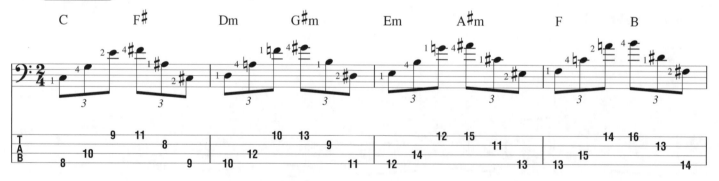

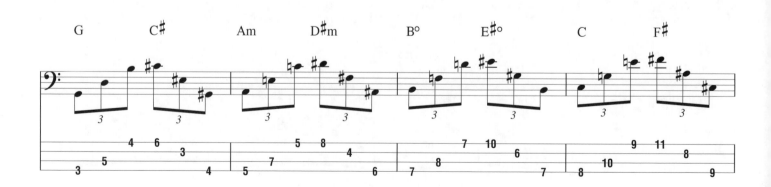

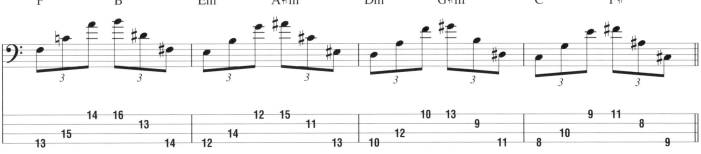

Seventh Chords

When we add a 3rd on top of a triad, we create a seventh chord. In the key of C, seventh chords stack up diatonically like this:

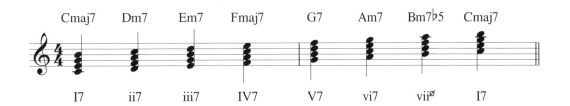

The I7 and IV7 chords in a major key are *major seventh chords*; the ii7, iii7, and vi7 chords are *minor seventh chords*; the V7 is a *dominant seventh* chord; and the vii7♭5 chord is a *minor seventh (flat five)* (or half-diminished) chord. The most common chord progression in jazz is the ii7–V7–I7 progression (Dm7–G7–Cmaj7 in the key of C). Memorize this progression in all keys. Most jazz standards can be broken down largely into ii–V–I progressions in different keys. If you have these progressions at your immediate beck and call, you can learn chord progressions to tunes in a quick and organized fashion.

As we continue to stack 3rds, we create 9th, 11th, and 13th chords. In terms of spelling, the 9th is the same as the 2nd degree of the scale, the 11th is the same as the 4th degree, and the 13th is the same as the 6th degree. Because of the wide variety of extensions used, we'll deal with dominant seventh chords in the next section.

Let's start with major seventh chords. These are built by adding a major 3rd on top of a major triad. Further extensions are added thusly:

*The 11th is sharped to create a
more common jazz harmony.

Notice that, as we stack 3rds, we actually create superimposed triads and seventh chords. For example, we could look at Cmaj9 as an Em7 over a C root, or Cmaj13 as a D major triad over Cmaj7. Approaching extended chords in this way will help you think harmonically outside the box and become less dependent on root-oriented patterns in your soloing. Start looking for these superimpositions as you practice.

Next up are the minor seventh chords, which are built by adding a minor 3rd to a minor triad. We can add further extensions to these as well:

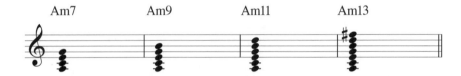

Applying the same idea as before, we see that Am9 can be viewed as a Cmaj7 chord over an A bass note, Am11 as G over an Am chord, and Am13 can be treated as B minor over Am7. The more you practice thinking this way, the more patterns you will see.

We proceed now to the major seventh (sharp five) and diminished seventh chords:

By placing a minor 3rd over an augmented triad, we get a major seventh (sharp five) chord. A minor 3rd added to a diminished triad yields a diminished seventh chord, while adding a major 3rd to that diminished triad gives us a minor seventh (flat five) chord, also known as a half-diminished chord. Diminished seventh chords, in particular, provide some interesting melodic possibilities due to the symmetry of stacking minor 3rds, so I have included some exercises with these to give you food for thought.

After the basic minor and major seventh arpeggios on the following pages, I have included an exercise Jaco wrote that alternates minor ninth chords with major seventh (sharp eleven) chords in a chromatic progression.

Feel free to invent your own exercises, and by all means explore alternate fingerings.

Major Seventh Chords

Cmaj7   Alternate position   Upper octave

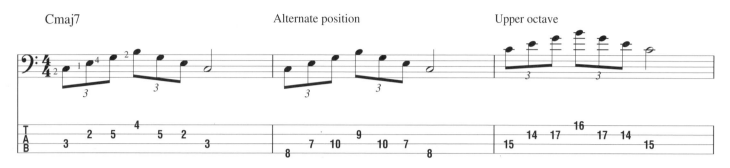

Two octaves

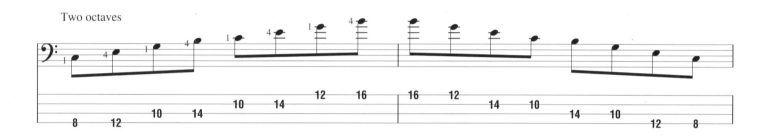

Cmaj9   Cmaj7♯11

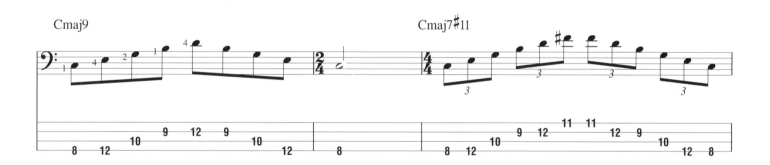

Cmaj13

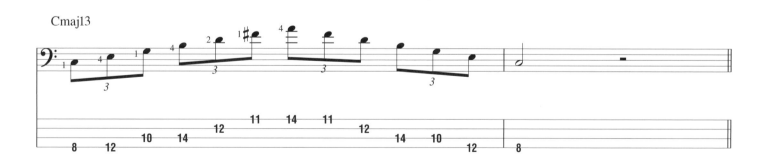

Minor Seventh Chords

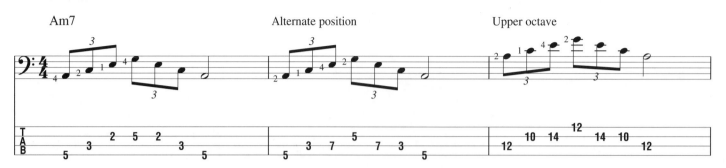

Am7   Alternate position   Upper octave

Two octaves

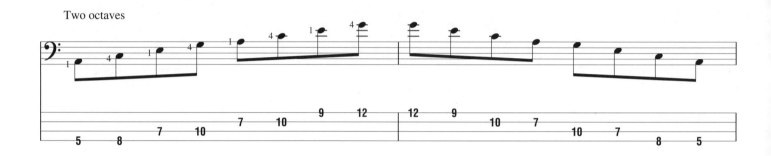

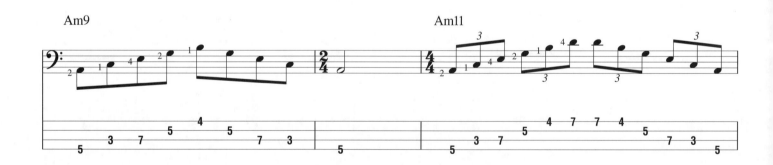

Am9   Am11

Am13

Alternating Minor Seventh/Major Seventh ♯11 Chords

 TRACK 9

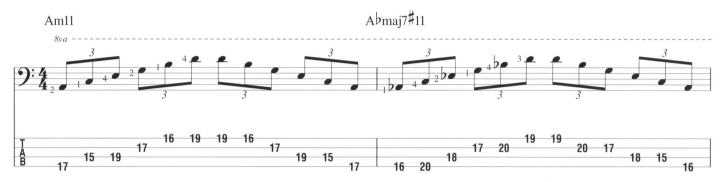

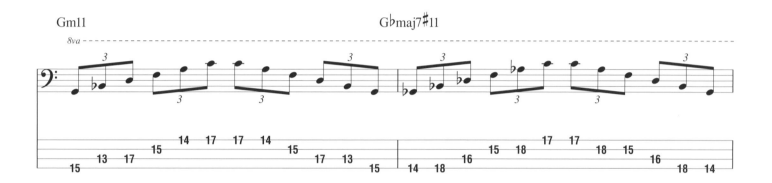

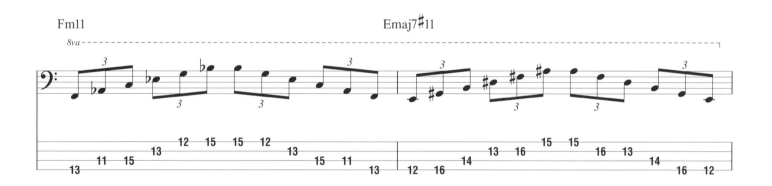

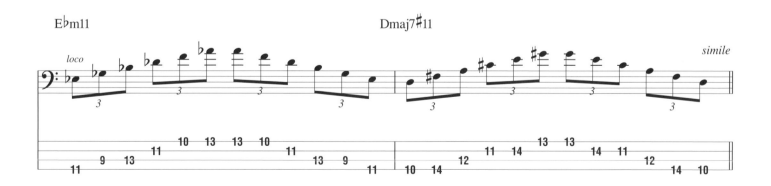

Major Seventh ♯5 Chords

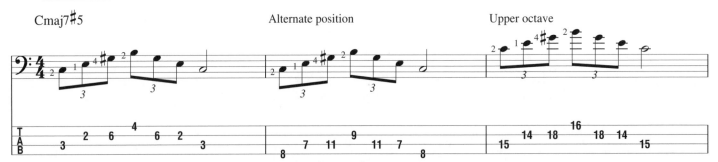

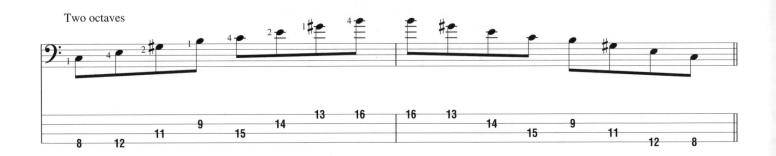

Diminished Seventh Chords

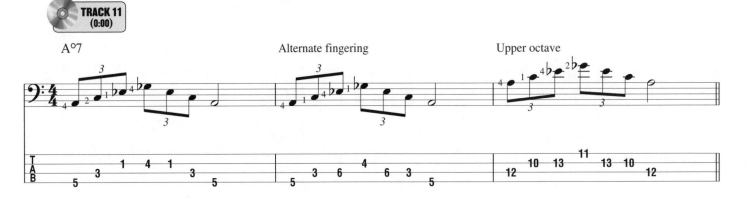

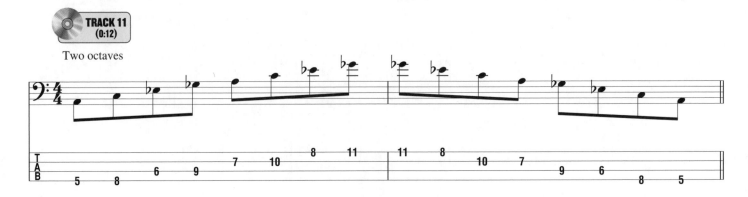

Am7♭5 (half-diminished)

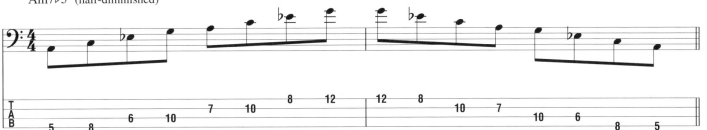

A°7

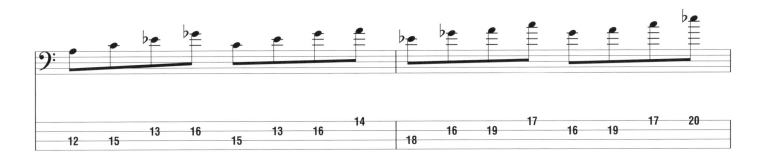

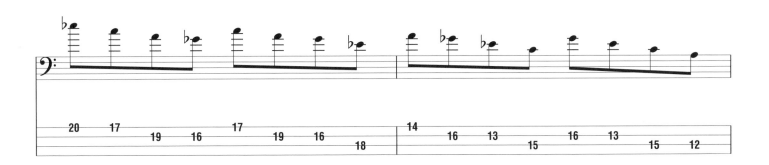

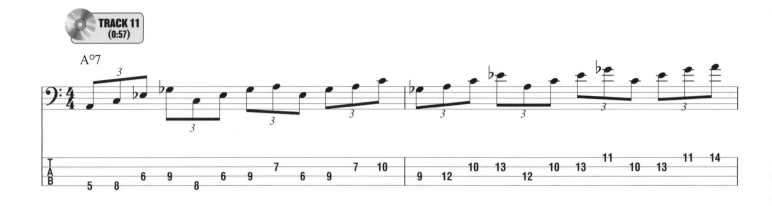

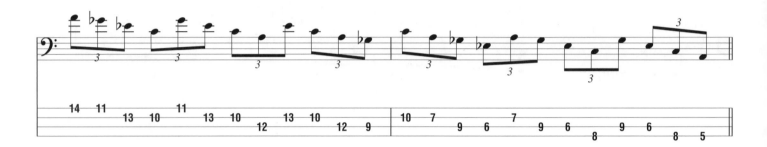

Dominant Seventh Chords

Congratulations on making it to where the action is—dominant seventh chords. The more you learn and practice dominant seventh chords and their extensions, the further you will go into a world of harmonic color and melodic chromaticism. First, let's look at the basic dominant seventh chord structures:

The ♭5th (tritone) interval between the 3rd (E) and ♭7th (B♭) gives the dominant seventh chord its characteristic feeling of harmonic tension. In the previous three examples, the only difference between the three chords is the 5th of the chord (5th, ♭5th, ♯5th, respectively). Let's examine some of the common extensions of the dominant seventh chords. After the ♭7th interval, we add the 9th, 11th, and 13th of the chord, successively:

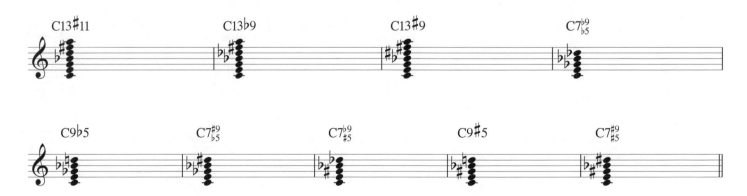

Once again, you can readily see how superimposed triads are created by adding 3rds to the original seventh chord. For example, C13♯11 can be broken down to D over C7. C13♭9 can be seen as a G♭ minor triad over C7. C7♯9♯5 can be interpreted as G♯ (A♭) over C7. This is a much simpler way of dealing with complex chord structures. Many of these superimpositions are easy to see when played in jazz piano voicings. A good jazz pianist would never play these chords in the fashion printed here, but you should learn to spell these chords from the bottom up. Once you are comfortable with spelling the seventh chords, add the 9th, 11th, and 13th intervals. The subject of jazz chord voicings is beyond the scope of this book, but I recommend you listen to the music of Bill Evans, Herbie Hancock, McCoy Tyner, Wynton Kelly, Oscar Peterson, and any of the other great jazz pianists in order to develop your ear for jazz chord voicings.

Extended dominant seventh chords lend themselves readily to tritone substitution, as we discussed earlier. Let's look at one example on the keyboard:

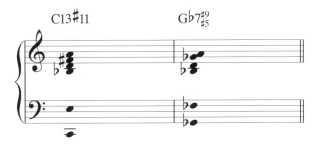

Although the spelling of the pitches is different (or, to put it correctly, *enharmonic*), the notes of both chords are the same except for the root. The tritone created by the 3rd and the ♭7th of the C13 chord (E and B♭) is mirrored in the G♭7 chord (F♭ and B♭), except their relationship to the root is reversed (3rd–♭7th in C becomes ♭7th–3rd in G♭). Where C7 would be the V7 chord in the key of F, G♭7 would be the ♭II7 in the key of F. This is one of the most common flat five substitutions you will encounter (♭II7 substituting for V7). As always, the more you practice these chords, both on your bass and at the keyboard, the more these relationships will become apparent to you. In your head, spell the V7 chord in any key, followed by the ♭II7 chord. Play this same exercise in all keys. In an actual playing situation, you have to be able to make these associations very quickly, so thorough memorization is essential.

In the following exercises, I have added the extensions one by one in order to facilitate learning each structure and to illustrate different fingering possibilities.

Dominant Seventh Chords

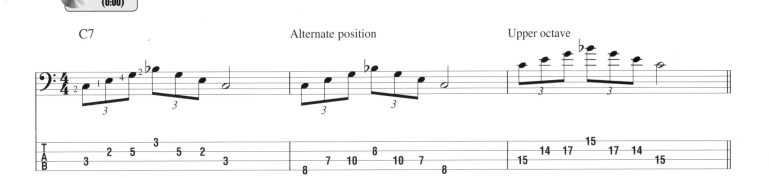

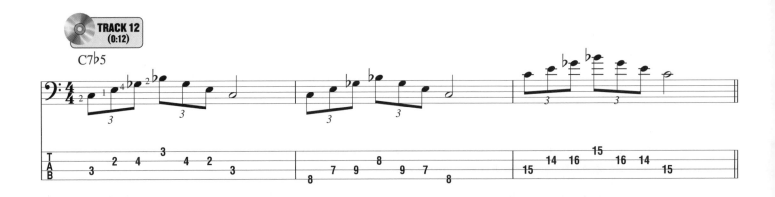

TRACK 12 (0:12)

C7♭5

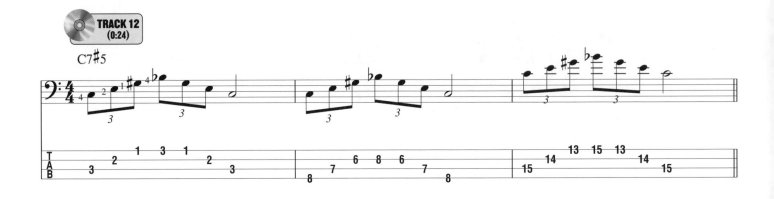

TRACK 12 (0:24)

C7♯5

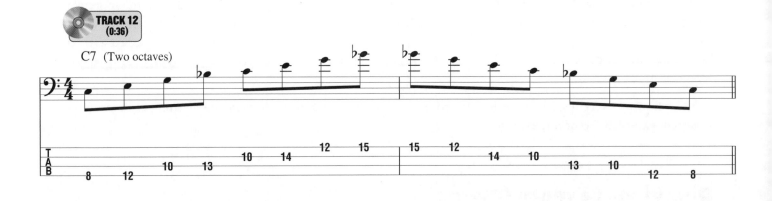

TRACK 12 (0:36)

C7 (Two octaves)

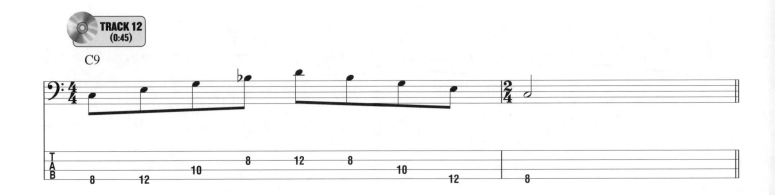

TRACK 12 (0:45)

C9

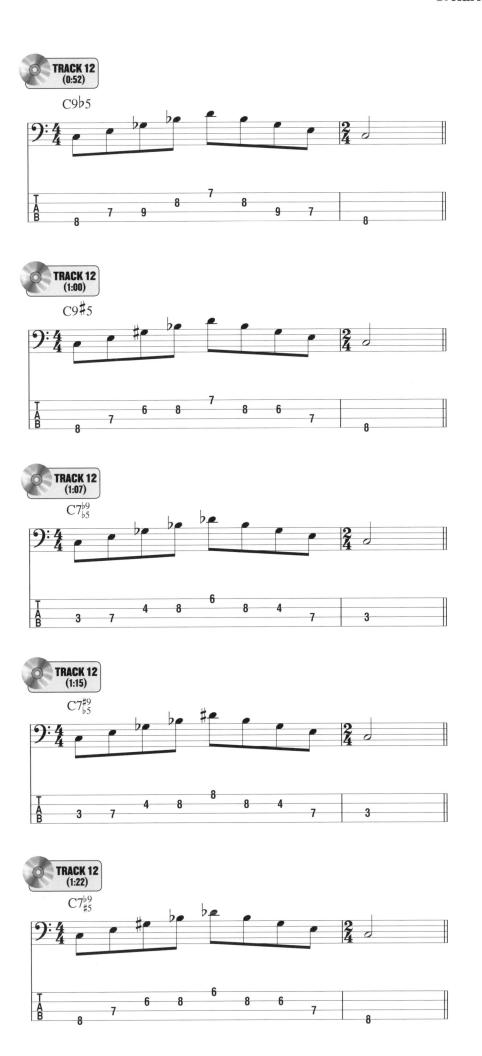

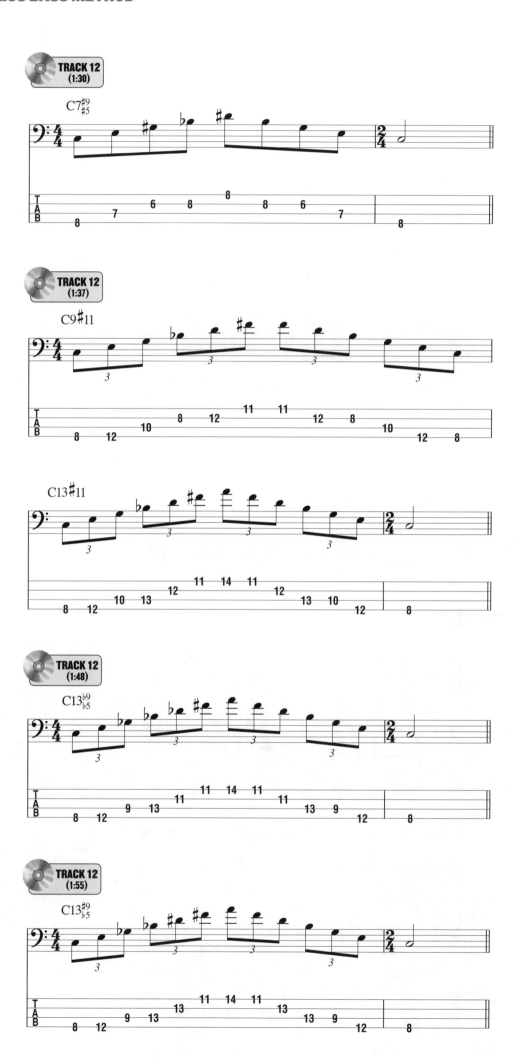

Diatonic Seventh Chords

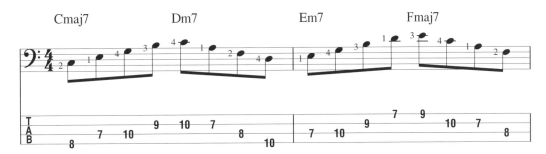

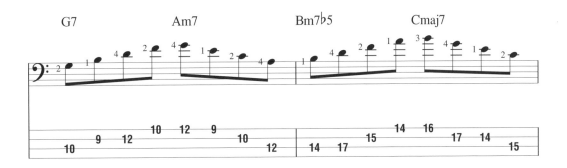

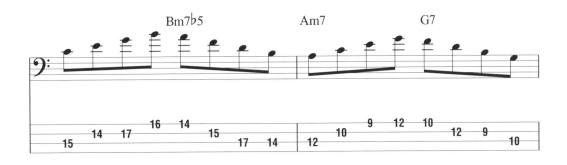

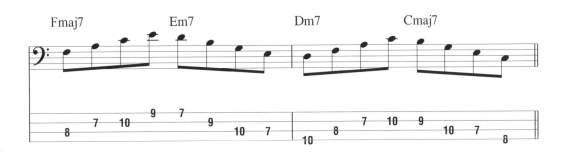

Harmonics

One of the most surprising elements the first time I heard and saw Jaco play was his use of harmonics. I had heard harmonics played on guitar and used them to tune up, but it had never occurred to me (or anyone else, apparently) to use them in a musical context on the bass. This was a classic example of a recurring theme in my studies with him ("Gee, why didn't I ever think of that?"). Such is the intensely-focused common sense of his genius.

As most bassists know, *natural harmonics* are played by lightly touching various points of the string without depressing the string to the fingerboard. Here's a chart showing the main natural harmonics you will find useful. The decimal points indicate those found *between* certain frets (as opposed to directly over the fret). The values are approximate; ears and hands are what matter here, so don't worry about purchasing a fret ruler. The (+) values found here indicate the number of octaves above the open string in addition to the interval sounded. The perceptive student will notice that the natural harmonics listed below from the twelfth to the second frets on any given string produce a dominant ninth chord whose root is the same as the open string. There are, of course, more harmonics available on the instrument. If you want to delve further, I suggest you acquire a book on bass harmonics and spend time experimenting.

Fret No.	Interval	Note Produced On:			
		E string	**A string**	**D string**	**G string**
1.7	Major 3rd (+3)	G♯	C♯	F♯	B
2	Major 2nd (+3)	F♯	B	E	A
2.2	Octave (+3)	E	A	D	G
2.7	Minor 7th (+2)	D	G	C	F
3	Perfect 5th (+2)	B	E	A	D
4 (9,16)	Major 3rd (+2)	G♯	C♯	F♯	B
5	Octave (+1)	E	A	D	G
6	Minor 7th	D	G	C	F
7 (19)	Perfect 5th (+1)	B	E	A	D
12	Octave	E	A	D	G

You can also produce *artificial harmonics* on the bass in one of two ways: One way is by lightly stopping the string with the thumb of your picking hand while you pluck the string with your first finger at various lengths of the string. You can discover these points by experimenting yourself. Learning to feel where those points are is more useful than a technical discussion (it's a touch thing). Jaco employed this technique to great success on Weather Report's "Birdland." This creates a very cool guitar-like effect, and it's a nice flavor to throw into your solos from time to time.

The other method of producing artificial harmonics is by actually holding down the string with the index finger and stretching up with your fourth finger to play the harmonic. This device, of course, was used by Jaco in his brilliant harmonics showcase, "Portrait of Tracy."

Portrait of Tracy

As if our minds weren't completely blown by hearing the solos on "Donna Lee," "Continuum," and "(Used to Be A) Cha-Cha" in rapid succession on his first album, we now had to adjust our brains to the reality of "Portrait of Tracy"—and this was only side one (yes, we're going back to the days of vinyl here)! Beyond the usual references one reads about the expansion of the instrument's vocabulary and technical difficulties, there is another facet of this piece that I find truly amazing. Here, as elsewhere, Jaco has created a work that is, for all its formidable technical challenges and advanced musical language, full of beautiful melody and soulful expression. Like other great masters, he makes the complex sound simple. There is certainly a lesson here in using technical resources and musical knowledge in the service of creating beautiful music and not merely to display one's technical prowess. Let's look at this work of genius:

The intro is a sequence that outlines Gmaj7–Dmaj7–Amaj7–E.

The main theme uses parallel major seventh chords with the major seventh at the strong points of the melody. This is similar to the harmony and melody of another one of Jaco's pieces, "Havona," which we will look at later. He alternates cadences here, ending first on Cmaj9, then on E♭7♯9. Jaco then plays a series of chords with chromatically descending motion in the bass, coming to a repeated figure that essentially prolongs the feeling of E7. This leads us into the 5/4 section. Here, he pedal tones double-stop harmonics in the melody, D and A, while alternating bass notes chromatically, C–B–B♭. This creates harmonic change (C–Bm7–B♭maj7) over the common melody notes. He then modulates to a variation on this sequence, A♭13♯11 to Gmaj7. After the cadence of B♭maj7–Fmaj7, he restates the first theme. He ends on Emaj7♯11.

Technical Note: In measure 4, Jaco produces artificial harmonics by holding down the second fret of the A string with his first finger while playing the harmonic on the sixth fret with his fourth finger. Similarly, he plays the final chord by holding down the ninth fret on the A, D, and G strings with the first finger while playing the harmonics on the thirteenth fret with the fourth finger.

Portrait of Tracy

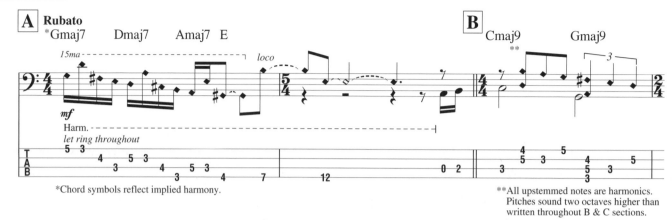

*Chord symbols reflect implied harmony.

**All upstemmed notes are harmonics. Pitches sound two octaves higher than written throughout B & C sections.

***D♯ harp harm. is produced by fretting B on the 2nd fret of the A string with the 1st finger, then playing the harmonic on the 6th fret with the 4th finger.

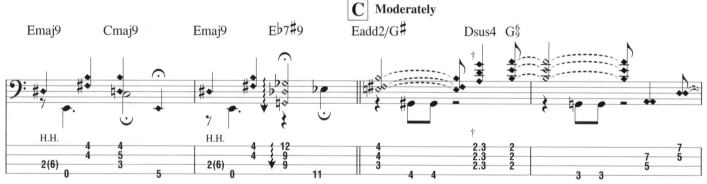

†Harmonic located 3/10 the distance between 2nd & 3rd frets.

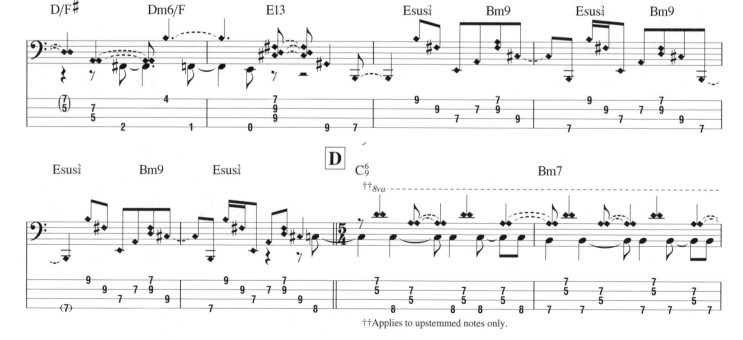

††Applies to upstemmed notes only.

By Jaco Pastorius
Copyright © 1976 Pastorius Music
Copyright Renewed
All Rights Reserved   Used by Permission

*Upstemmed notes sound two octaves higher than written to end.

**Harp harm. played by barring 9th fret with the index finger and extending fourth finger to the 13th fret.

35

4. Melodic Elements

"You can play practically any note; it's just a matter of understanding how they work together."

For all the jaw-dropping technical virtuosity that permeated Jaco's work, he never lost sight of the most basic element of music: *melody*. Classic examples like his playing on Weather Report's "Cannonball," "A Remark You Made," or his own "Continuum," readily come to mind in this regard. Jaco knew how to make the bass sing. This is one of the characteristics that gave his music such broad appeal. On various recorded examples of his live solo spots with Weather Report and Joni Mitchell, as well as in his own shows, you can hear him quote melodies like "The Sound of Music," the theme from *The High and the Mighty*, the theme from *The Carol Burnett Show*, Hindemith's Op. 50, *Concert Music for Strings and Brass*, Wayne Shorter's "Dolores," Jimi Hendrix's "Third Stone from the Sun," and of course, "America the Beautiful."

In our discussions, Jaco would frequently cite television as a big influence on his musical sensibilities. While this may at first seem rather humorous, I'll never forget the time guitarist Randy Bernsen and I were sitting in Jaco's living room watching "The Three Stooges." While we were busy laughing every time Moe would poke Curly in the eye or hit him over the head, Jaco was busy pointing out what instrumental device was being employed to create the accompanying sound effect (pizzicato violin in the case of the eye-poking, I believe). Jaco's mind was always on music, one way or another. I feel the lesson here is that music is all around us, if our ears are in tune.

As bassists, it's easy for us to get musically lazy and forget to extend our musical awareness beyond the bass part. Jaco always stressed learning the melody to every tune. Playing melodically transcends merely playing scales up and down the neck. By practicing melodies, we learn to use intervals and develop phrasing. The rhythmic value of the notes we play and the rests between notes give our lines musical shape and substance. While playing exercises is extremely important in developing our solo skills, making musical *statements* is the ultimate goal of our practice. I'm stressing this now because we're about to embark on the practicing of scales. Learning scales is not only essential in building up dexterity on the instrument but serves as a guide to what combinations of notes work over various chords. Practice them diligently, but try to avoid the tendency to endlessly run scales in your soloing.

In the examples that follow, I include a trick that I learned from Jaco. Scales are usually taught in one or two octaves. While I have included these, I have also included what I have labeled as "extended" scales. Jaco showed me how he liked to practice scales up to the point on the G string where another shift in position would be required. This would generally stop short of two octaves. You will find, as I did, that playing scales in this fashion is a tremendous way of building speed, especially in your right hand, since it takes you straight across the strings and back. When practicing scales, start at a comfortable tempo and strive for smoothness in your articulation of the notes. Pick a tempo at which you can play every note evenly without stumbling. *Keep the tempo steady.* Once you develop even articulation at a steady tempo, you will find it much easier to play scales faster. Avoid the tendency to try playing like a bat out of hell while fluffing over the notes. "First you have to play it legitimately," as Jaco would say. It's also a good idea to practice scales with the chords over which they work best. For example, play the Dorian mode with minor seventh chords, whole tone scales with augmented chords, etc. After the following pages of scales and intervals, you will find three exercises of melodic sequences that Jaco taught me. These figured prominently in our studies. Learn them in all keys.

Major Scales

Major Scales

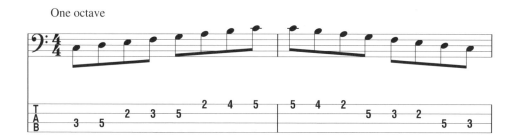

One octave

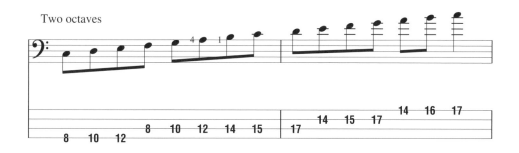

Two octaves

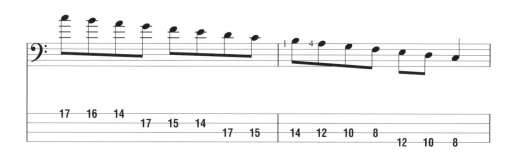

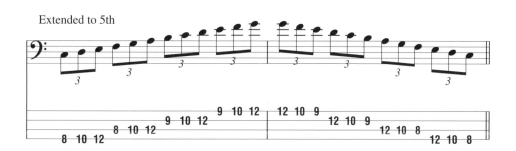

Extended to 5th

Minor Scales

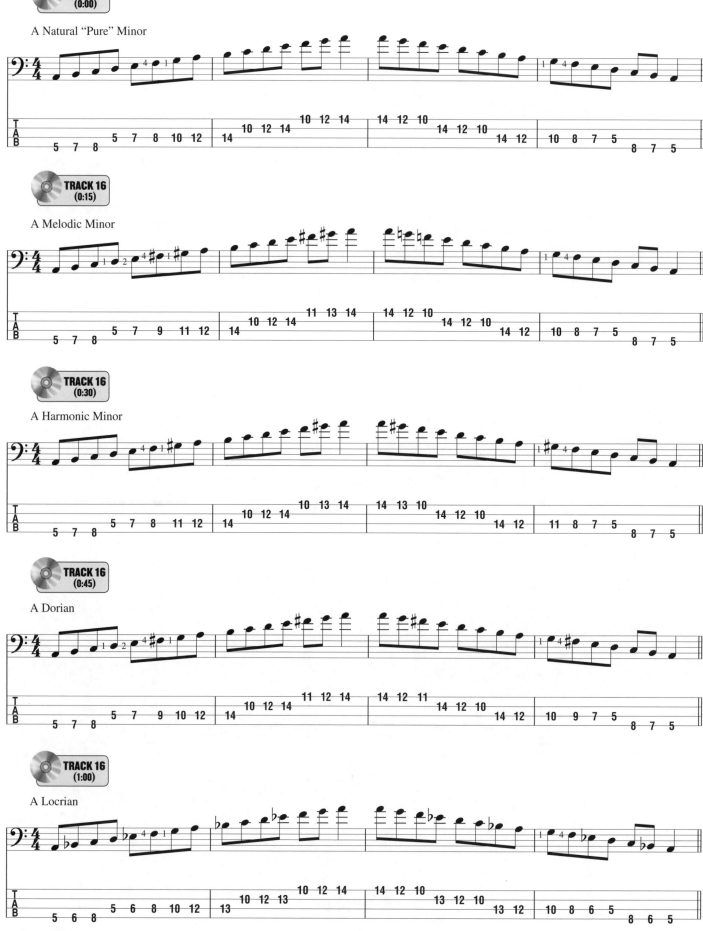

Whole Tone Scale

One octave

Two octaves

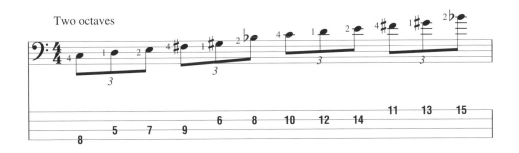

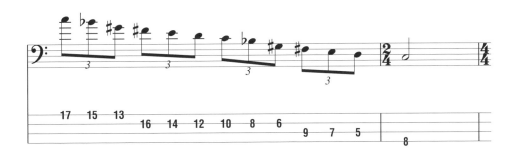

Extended

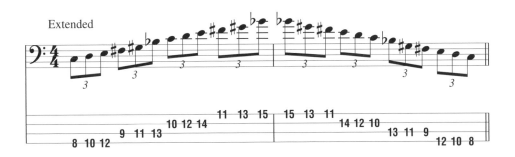

Diminished Scale

One octave

Two octaves

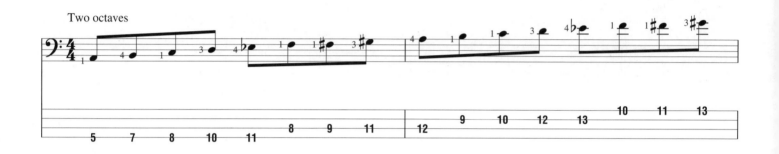

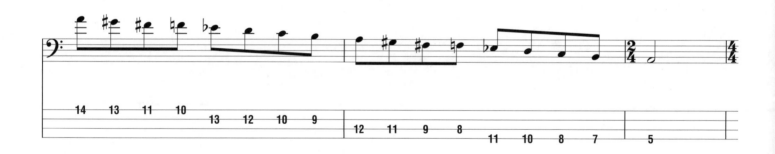

Extended

Major Pentatonic Scale

One octave

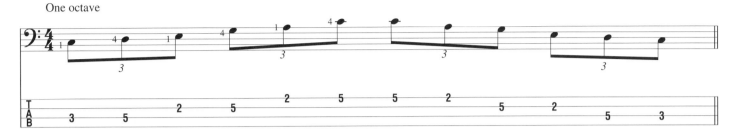

TRACK 19 (0:06)

Two octaves

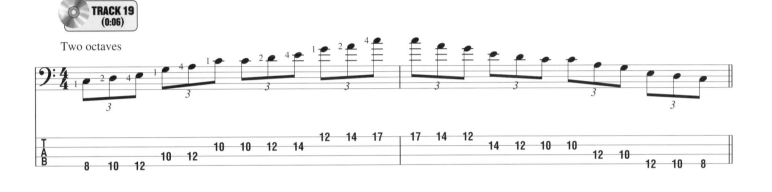

TRACK 19 (0:15)

Extended

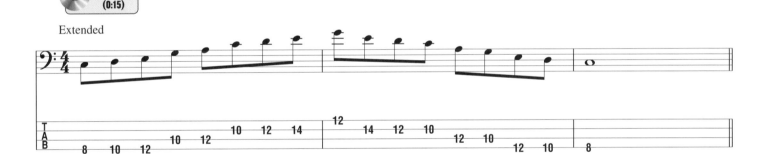

Minor Pentatonic Scale

TRACK 20 (0:00)

One octave

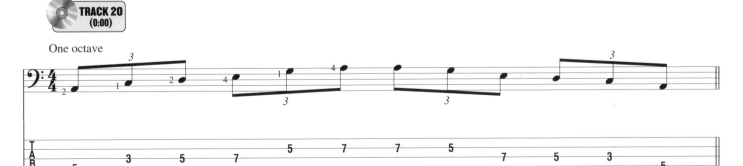

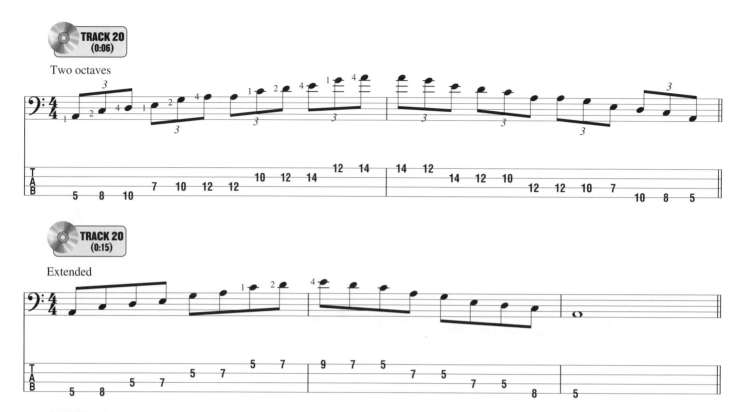

Modes

Modes are resources you will draw from time and again in your playing. We often hear the term "modal" in reference to tunes like Miles Davis's "So What" or John Coltrane's "Impressions," both of which are based on the Dorian mode. *Modes* can be thought of in one of two ways:

- **They can be seen as scales derived from the major scale.** For example, D Dorian can be thought of as a C major scale starting and ending on D, the 2nd degree. F *Lydian* can be interpreted as a C major scale starting and ending on the 4th degree (F), and so on.

- **They can be viewed as major or minor scales.** Taking the Dorian mode again, we can think of it as a "pure" minor scale with a raised 6th. The Lydian mode can also be seen as a major scale with a ♯4th.

In the interest of conciseness, I have only given a two-octave version of the modes here. Practice them in the same way as the other scales—i.e., one-octave, two-octave, and extended patterns in all keys.

The following table provides both views of the modes, along with their most common harmonic usage. The "Scale Degree" column gives you the note of the "parent" major scale that the mode starts on, while the "Scale Interpretation" column gives you the interpretation of the mode as a scale unto itself. The "Chordal Context" column gives you the most common harmonic usage of the particular mode.

Mode	Scale Degree	Scale Interpretation	Chordal Context
Ionian	I	Same as major scale	Major triad, maj7
Dorian	ii	"Pure" minor w/ raised 6th	m7
Phrygian	iii	"Pure" minor w/ ♭2nd	"Spanish" minor flavor
Lydian	IV	Major with ♯4th	maj7
Mixolydian	V	Major with ♭7th	Dominant 7
Aeolian	vi	Same as "pure" minor	m7
Locrian	vii	"Pure" minor w/ ♭2nd and ♭5th	min7♭5

Modes

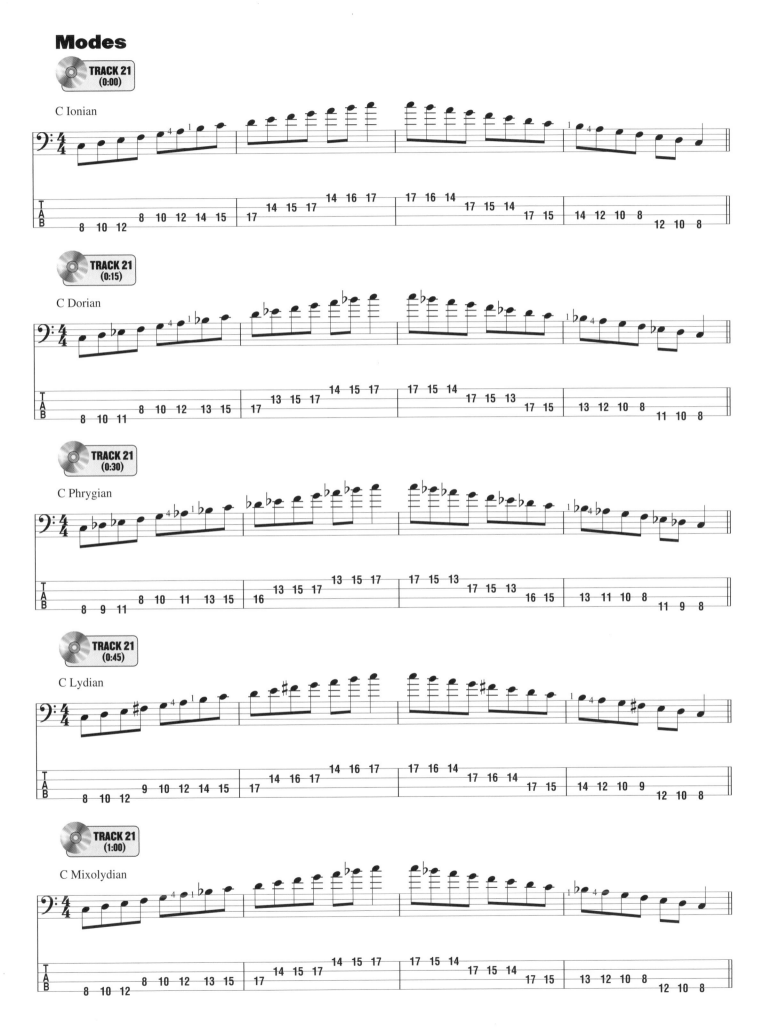

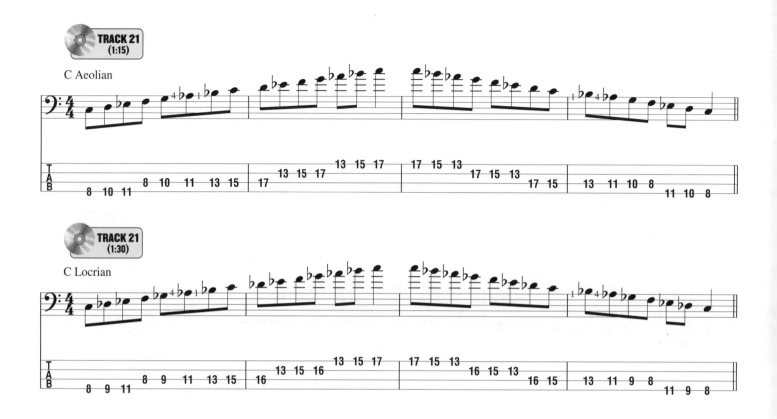

Dominant Seventh Scales

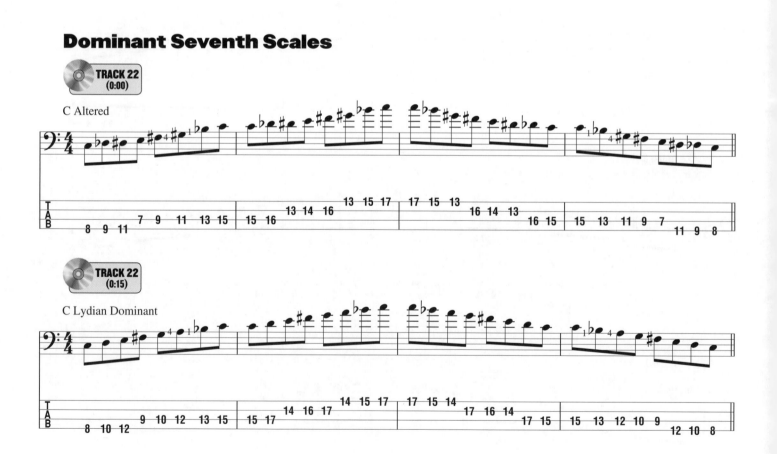

TRACK 22 (0:30)

C Lydian Augmented (start on 3, ♭5, ♯5, ♭7, or ♭9 of chord)

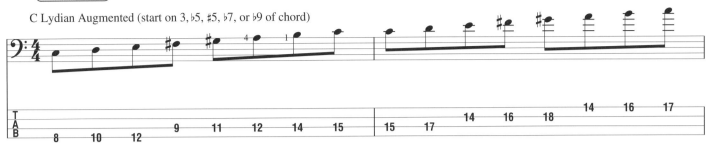

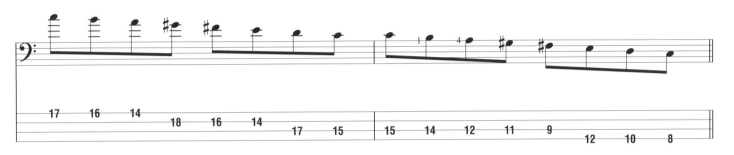

TRACK 22 (0:45)

C Blues

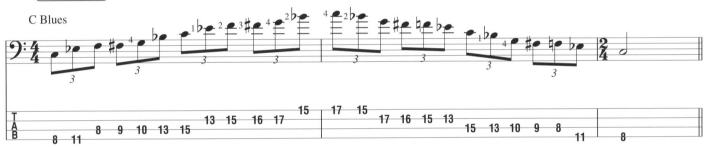

TRACK 22 (0:55)

Auxiliary Diminished

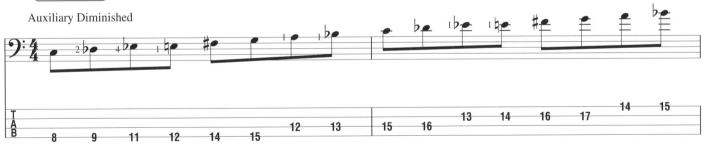

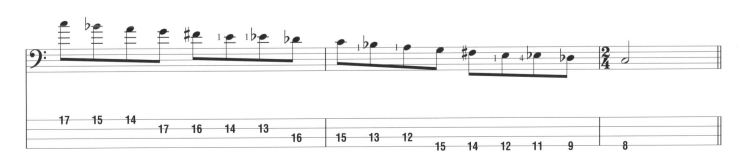

Diatonic Intervals

Thirds

Fourths

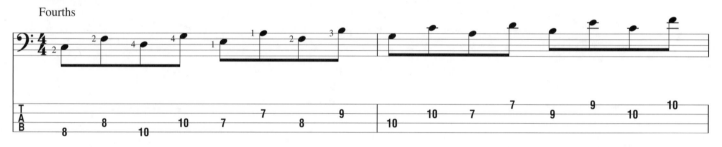

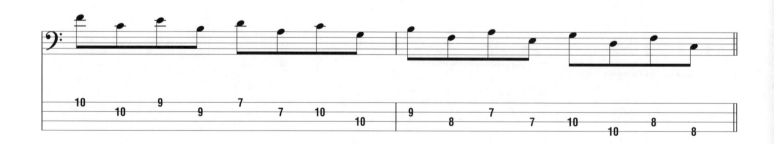

Fifths

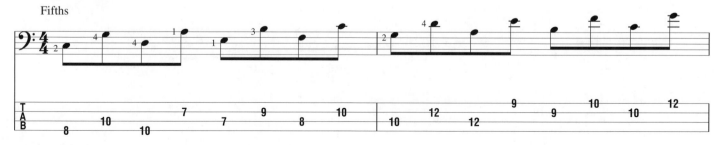

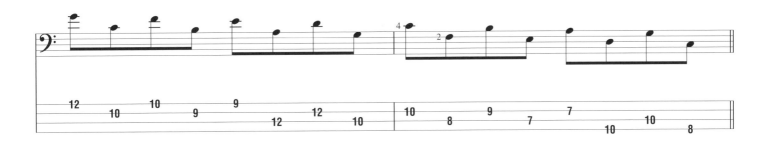

TRACK 23
(0:45)

Sixths

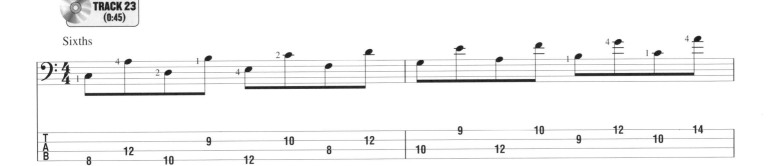

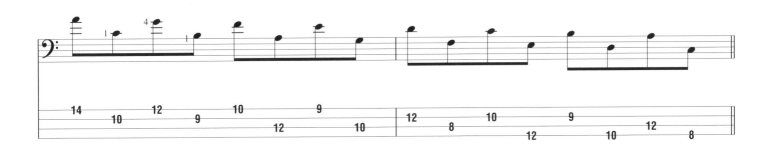

TRACK 23
(1:00)

Sevenths

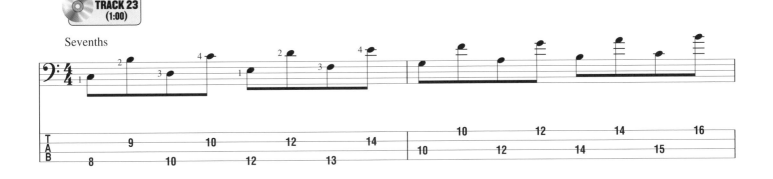

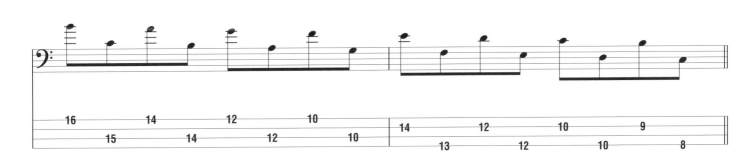

Melodic Sequence 1

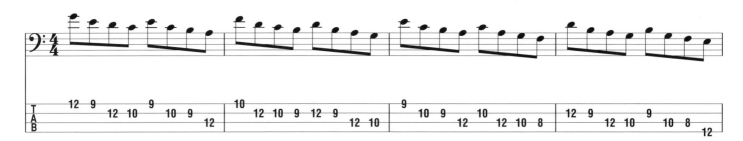

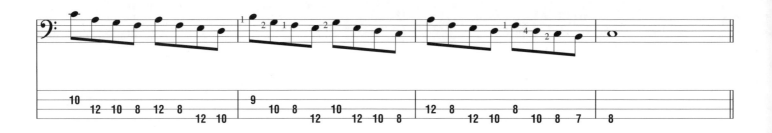

Melodic Sequence 2

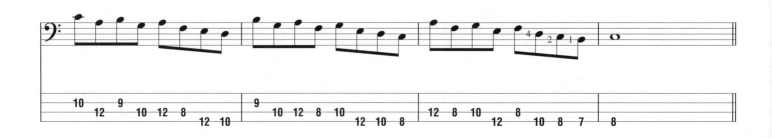

Melodic Sequence 3

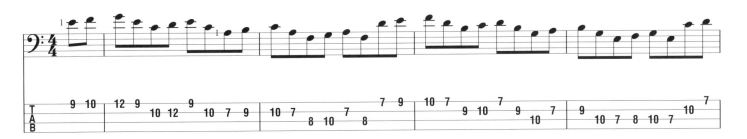

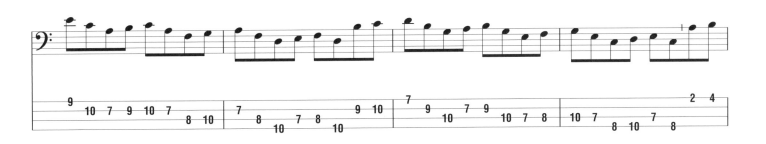

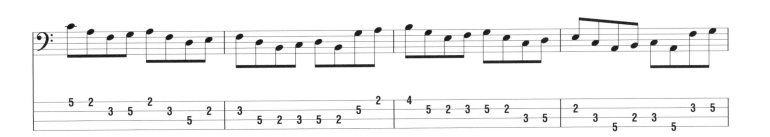

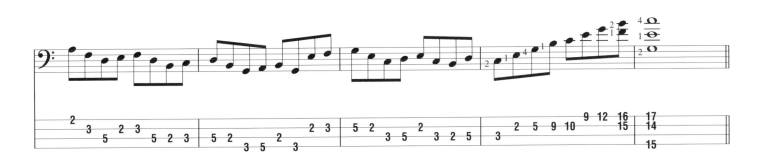

Turnarounds

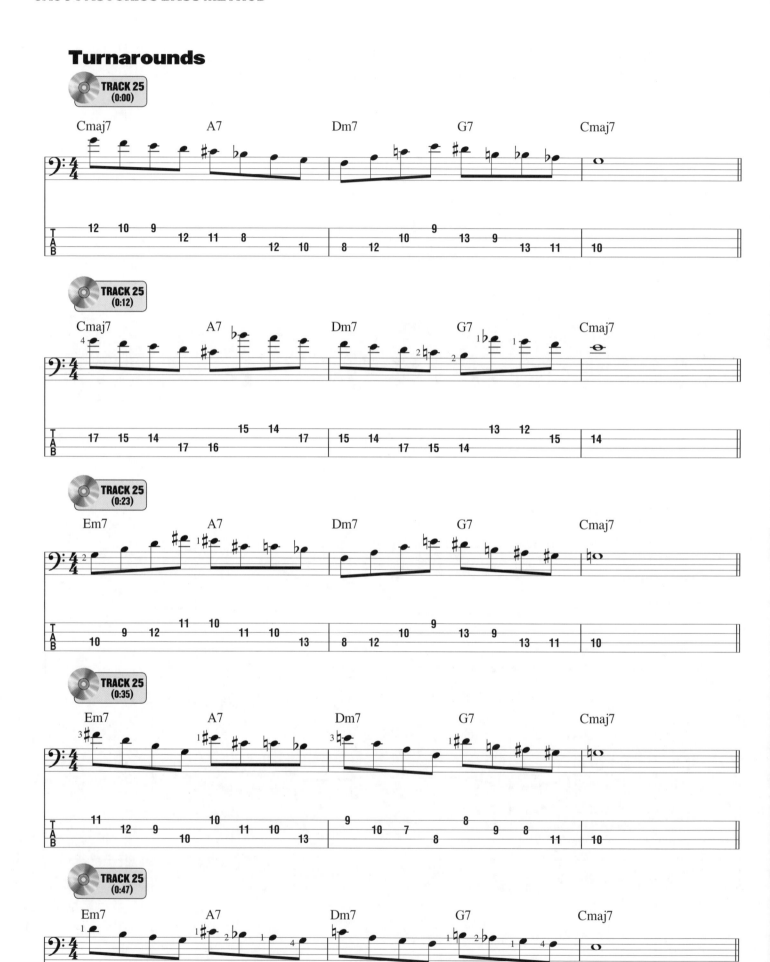

5. Rhythmic Elements

"You can't force music; it's just gonna happen."

Jaco was not merely the world's greatest bass soloist; he was a giant among men rhythmically as well. Even though his style stands out for the density of its content, there is never any question as to where the rhythmic pulse is at any given moment. Feel was always of paramount importance to Jaco.

If you wish to gain a deeper understanding of the rhythmic component of Jaco's playing, a good starting point would undoubtedly be a thorough study of the music of James Brown. Jaco was an absolute scholar of James Brown's music. As a fan of the "Godfather of Soul" myself, I was delighted to learn this about Jaco during the course of my studies. At the beginning of one of my lessons, he pulled out a *Maceo* album and put it on for our enjoyment. I also recall Jaco playing me his copy of the live album he recorded with Albert Mangelsdorf and saying, "Listen to this part—the whole band sounds like James Brown!" while smiling broadly. He liked to call off JB's "Sex Machine" when he and I would jam together at clubs. To put it simply, it is impossible to separate the influence of James Brown and soul music from Jaco's music. Let the truly wise student govern his listening habits accordingly.

The southern school of R&B, as represented by such artists as Otis Redding, Sam & Dave, Clarence Carter, Arthur Conley, Wilson Pickett, Joe Tex, Aretha Franklin, Little Beaver, et al., had a seminal influence on Jaco's art. His early professional experiences playing at the Downbeat Club, and with Woodchuck, Tommy Strand and the Upper Hand, and, of course, with Wayne Cochran & the C.C. Riders, forged a rhythm & blues edge in Jaco's playing that would make itself felt throughout his entire career.

The second cut on his debut album, *Jaco Pastorius*, features Sam & Dave on a tune written with one of Jaco's creative partners from the early R&B days, Bob Herzog, entitled "Come On, Come Over." He starts out with a line that combines his trademark staccato sixteenth notes with sustained resting points on the tonic in a characteristic "question and answer" style bass line.

Come On, Come Over

By Jaco Pastorius and Bob Herzog
Copyright © 1976 Pastorius Music and Bob Herzog Publishing
Copyright Renewed
All Rights Reserved   Used by Permission

In the bridge section, Jaco creates a feeling of acceleration by bringing on the sixteenth notes. Note how he slurs the last sixteenths of beats 3 and 4 to create a heightened sense of forward motion.

As a fellow south Floridian, I can attest to the fact that one of the great things about the music scene there at that time was the influence from the various cultures of the Caribbean. Reggae, calypso, and Cuban music, in particular, were strongly felt, and Jaco made tremendous use of all of these in his music. On the cut "Opus Pocus," he starts with one such influence: reggae.

Opus Pocus

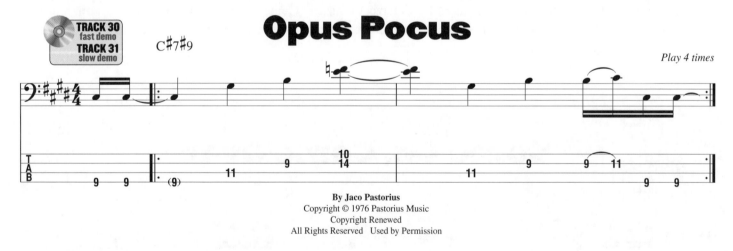

By Jaco Pastorius

The second groove, in E major, maintains the island flavor, but leans in more of an R&B direction, complete with Jaco's characteristic sixteenth notes.

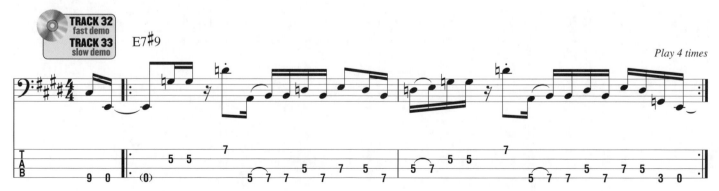

In the third groove (B♭7), the sixteenth-note R&B flavor becomes even stronger:

Jaco uses double stops to create a bass line reminiscent of a James Brown rhythm guitar part on the big band gem from his *Word of Mouth* album, "Liberty City." Here, he actually creates the effect of two parts: bass and rhythm guitar.

Liberty City

By Jaco Pastorius
Copyright © 1981 Mowgli Publishing
All Rights Reserved   Used by Permission

Some of Jaco's bass lines seem to straddle the world between R&B and another of his great loves, Afro-Cuban music. An early example of this is his work on Little Beaver's "I Can Dig It Baby."

I Can Dig It Baby

Compare the above line to both the next example, taken from the song "Kuru," and the E major groove in "Opus Pocus." The use of sixteenth notes, slurs in anticipation of the next beat, and the question-answer style are all here.

Kuru

On "(Used To Be A) Cha-Cha," Jaco doubles up on the cha-cha feel to relentlessly push the groove.

(Used to Be A) Cha-Cha

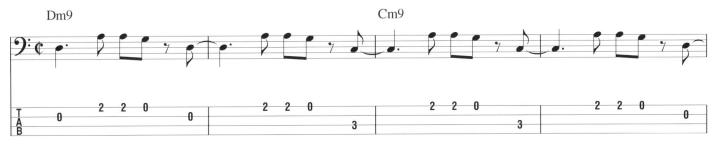

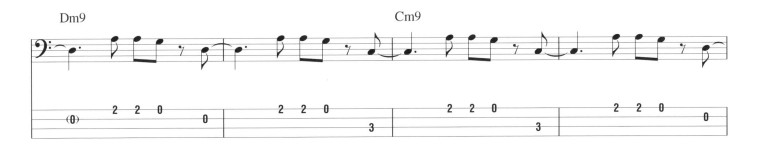

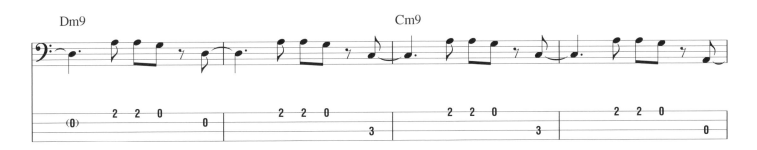

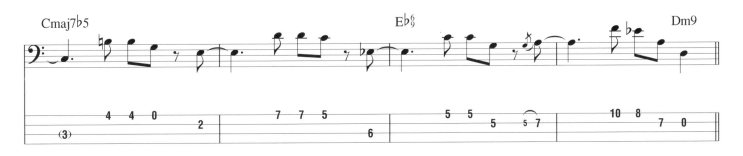

By Jaco Pastorius
Copyright © 1976 Pastorius Music
Copyright Renewed
All Rights Reserved   Used by Permission

Another example of Latin influence is found in the harmonics groove on "Okonkole Y Trompa." Both this and the previous groove are testimonials to Jaco's incredible stamina and ability to hold down the fort at any tempo as long as needed.

Okonkole Y Trompa

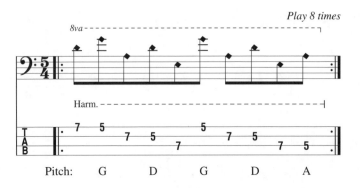

There is a tendency among some bassists who want to push the boundaries of the role and techniques of bass playing to forsake the groove aspect of the bass. These individuals obviously aren't paying close enough attention to Jaco's art (among other things). Although Jaco's approach to rhythm was unique, he was thoroughly grounded in the basics of funk, jazz, and Latin music where groove was concerned. He started out as a drummer, and it shows through in his playing as well. Take a tip from the master and absorb the necessary rhythmic influences through intensive listening and practice. Above all, go for the *feel*.

6. Soloistic Elements

At this point, you've rendered yourself "superbad" by memorizing every chord and scale known to man at lightning speed. You've mastered the previous examples of Jaco's grooves. You, the exemplary student, now stand ready to tackle the solo work of the great maestro. We will look at several examples taken from some of Jaco's most celebrated solos. I will break down the sections into analyses of how Jaco imposed his melodic thinking onto the chord changes.

After I had been studying with him for some time, he pulled out a spiral-bound manuscript with several of his solos written out, talking me through some of it while we sat at the piano. I never went to lessons hoping to "cop his licks," and I really appreciated him spontaneously opening the door to his work in this way. It gave me a lot of insight into how he looked at melody and harmony in his own solo work. It is my goal to pass this knowledge on to you. The analysis tables will enable you to quickly cross-reference the sections of the solo by measure numbers and chord changes. Outside of a few minor differences, most of the following transcriptions are based on Jaco's personal transcriptions in his own writing. I wish to thank Bob Bobbing and the Pastorius Family Library for giving me access to these manuscripts. In some cases, my hearing of certain passages did not agree entirely with Jaco's own transcriptions. In nearly all such cases, I deferred to Jaco's interpretation, for obvious reasons.

When I give degree numbers in the following analyses, they generally refer to the intervals relative to the root of the particular chord in question—not the overall key of the piece. This is the method Jaco used to explain his solos to me. As there are several transcription books of his solos already available, we will mainly be taking excerpts for analysis here. As you will readily see, there is no shortage of material to study in even one chorus of one of his solos. The exception is "Chromatic Fantasy," which I feel needs to be approached in its entirety.

While studying his solos in written form is definitely to be encouraged, I strongly suggest that you purchase transcription software and begin to transcribe for yourself if you are not already doing so. It's hard to beat transcribing for ear training and deepening your understanding of the music. I use *Transcribe!* by Seventh String Software (thanks to Pat Metheny for the tip on his website). If only I'd had this program when I was a young upstart! Do not blindly accept my analyses as scientific truth or as the ultimate arbiter in all matters pertaining to Jaco's solos. Analyze the passages for yourself and strive to gain your own insights into the music. This will help shape your growth as a musician.

Donna Lee

By the time the opening track ends at 2:27 into his debut album, Jaco Pastorius has completely shattered any conception as to what the bass guitar can do. It was certainly a revelation to me when he played it for me at his house before its release (one of the many perks of being his student). Like John Coltrane's "Giant Steps" or Eddie Van Halen's "Eruption," the history of the instrument (and the definition of virtuosity thereupon) was rewritten with this one piece. The speed, articulation, and phrasing in Jaco's solo sent all of us scurrying back to the woodshed. Besides taking on the melodic role normally associated with a horn player, Jaco also injects chordal elements, as well as interacting with the congas as if he were a percussionist with his driving, staccato phrasing. Following Jaco's example, I can't recommend strongly enough that the student saturate his ears and mind with the music of Charlie Parker. Learning Bird's tunes will really take you all over the instrument while providing an endless source of melodic and harmonic nourishment. Submitted here is an analysis of the first sixteen measures of Jaco's solo, starting with the two-measure pickup.

Donna Lee - Analysis

Measure #	Chord	Analysis
Pickup	Abmaj7–Bbm7–Eb7	Ab major triad arpeggiated, followed by Db major walkup into descending Ab major arpeggio.
1	Abmaj7	Plays 6th–3rd–9th of Ab major, then walks down scale from the 5th of Ab major into next chord.
2	F7	3rd to b9th of F7, followed by a lead-in figure to next chord.
3–4	Bb7	Plays the b7th to the 13th (Ab–G) leading into a descending C major triad (13th–#11th–9th), which resolves to the 3rd (D). He then plays an E7#9 chord with harmonics. The E7#9 chord is a tritone (b5) substitution of Bb7. Last notes in measure 4 begin diminished scale run.
5–6	Bbm7–Eb7	Continuation of diminished scale run.
7	Abmaj7	C minor arpeggio with walkdown to the 3rd (C) of the Abmaj7 chord.
8	Ebm7–D7	A ii–V pattern.
9–10	Dbmaj7–Dbm7	Jaco plays the 3rd and 7th of Dbmaj7, followed by E and Gb, implying movement to Gb7 (IV–bVII), over the Dbm7 chord. Notice the use of syncopation to break up the run of eighth notes immediately preceding. Descending chromatic motion down to the next chord.
11	Abmaj7	9th of the Abmaj7 chord leads into descending Cm7 arpeggio.
12	F7	Descending Eb diminished scale. Notice that the pickup note he plays in the previous measure (D) is omitted in the descending scale.
13–14	Bb7	Jaco's phrases become more chromatic toward the end of this chorus. The movement in measure 13 seems to imply G7 to Cm (G7 to F7). In measure 14, he roughly spells out Bbm(maj7) over the Bb7, ending on the b5th.
15–16	Bbm7–Eb7	After leading in with a C minor arpeggio, Jaco plays a pattern alternating a descending minor pentatonic figure with a descending minor seventh arpeggio. He plays this through Eb minor, Ab minor, and Db minor, substituting an E major triad on the last arpeggio, finally resolving to the 5th of the tonic chord (Eb).

Donna Lee

By Charlie Parker

Continuum

On Jaco's debut album, the bebop hipness of "Donna Lee" and the urban funk of the second track "Come On, Come Over" is followed by our first glimpse at Jaco's lyrical side in the form of the beautiful "Continuum." Fear not, shredders! For all its lyrical quality and feeling of open space, "Continuum" is chock-full of dense technical passages. The open, slow-moving harmony is juxtaposed with both melodically-expressive and rapid scale passages. Jaco's use of double stops and octaves is used to great effect here. The pentatonic basis of the tune alternates with more complex movement. Despite the technical difficulties presented by this piece (surprise!), the feeling of expansive, impressionistic beauty dominates throughout. I feel that this piece offers a glimpse into Jaco's love of both contemporary classical music and southern R&B stylings. You can hear the latter in the frequent use of hammer-ons when playing minor 3rds. It is a testimonial to Jaco's genius that he was consistently able to take such seemingly disparate styles and combine them into a fresh statement that retained the unmistakable stamp of his originality. At least in part, it is this combination of familiarity and innovation that gives his music such immediacy.

Continuum - Analysis

Measure #	Chord	Analysis
1–2	E_9^6	Begins with an E major pentatonic riff, emphasizing the 6th and 9th, then heads down the E major triad, resolving to the major 7th.
3–4	E_9^6	After playing a few low E notes for accompaniment, Jaco plays a lick that implies the V chord (B) over Emaj7, ending with a trill on D#, the 3rd of B. The following triplet phrase gives a Lydian sound by incorporating the #4th (A#) on its walkdown to G#. He ends this passage with a pentatonic run up to the next chord.
5–6	A_9^6	Jaco comes to rest briefly on the 3rd (C#) of the A_9^6 chord in measure 5, moving up to the 6th (F#) in measure 6. He repeats these two notes as a pickup into the next chord.
7–12	E_9^6	Jaco begins on the major 7th (D#) of the E chord—note the repeated use of this tonal color—and continues up the Emaj7 arpeggio. Measure 9 starts with a walkdown to an F# major triad. This gives us both the E_9^6 flavor and the Lydian sound of the A#. Jaco follows this with consecutive perfect 5ths (root–5th–9th–6th–3rd–7th) in measures 10–11. The following descending motif implies a C#m9 chord over the E tonal center, while yet again emphasizing the #4th (A#). He rests briefly on the 6th (C#), and a brief C# minor run leads into the next chord.
13	B♭m7	Begins with a descending passage that outlines a D♭maj7 chord. The A implies a dominant chord (F7) leading into B♭m7, which is expressed in a series of ascending perfect 5ths.
14	Am9	A C major triad is played before walking down to the root note (A). The end of the measure outlines Cmaj9.
15–16	E_9^6	After briefly resting on the 3rd (G#), Jaco plays a figure highlighting the 6th and 9th. In measure 16 he plays a C#m9 arpeggio.
17	E♭m7	Here Jaco begins a series of double stops. First, a D♭ double stop resolves to G♭, beginning a series of 3rds descending diatonically (Fm–E♭m–D♭). The last one resolves down a half step to the next chord.
18	Dm7	This measure is a series of double stops played over the open D string. The first is a 3rd (C), leading into three consecutive 6ths (F–Am–C). This passage outlines Fmaj7 over the Dm7 chord.
19	A_9^6	After starting a new chord with the 3rd (C#) underpinned by the open root (A) below, Jaco plays 7–6–5 resolving down to an F minor lick, then walks down to the next chord.
20	Cmaj7	Starts with a major 7th interval and resolves it to the 6th. He leads into the next chord with an Em7 run.
21	E_9^6	Begins on major 7th, then to the 9th, and resolves on the major 6th.

Continuum

Moderately

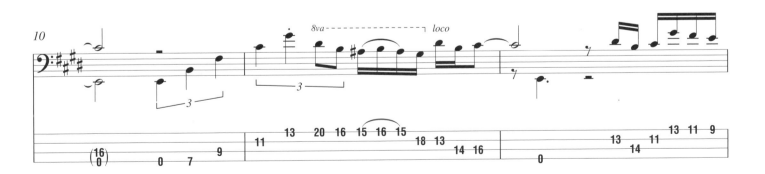

By Jaco Pastorius

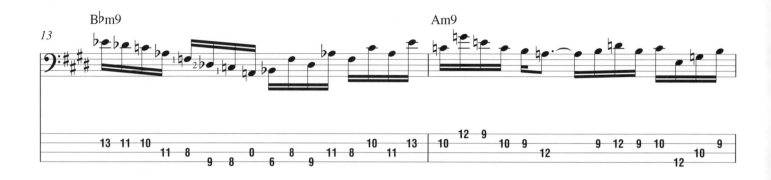

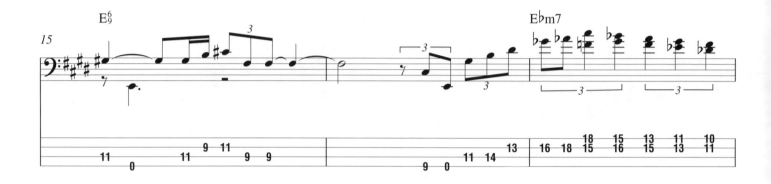

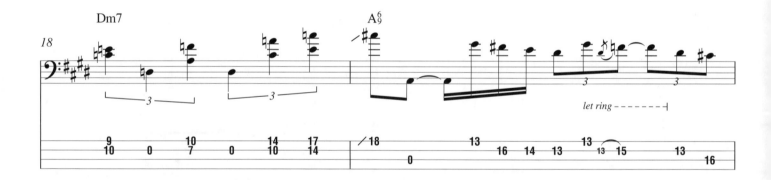

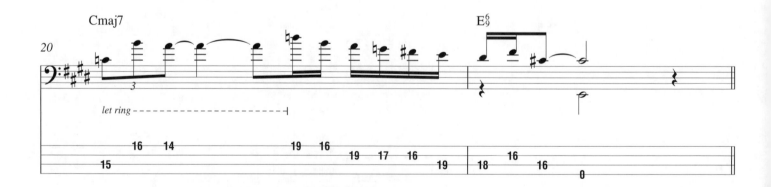

(Used to Be A) Cha-Cha

I remember Jaco putting a bass part in front of me early in our studies. It was a cut-time Latin part, entitled "Cha-Cha." Some months later, after his first album had been out for a while, he explained to me that, after he recorded the track, someone had asked what the title was. Jaco replied, "Cha-Cha." Herbie Hancock interjected with something like, "Man, that *used* to be a cha-cha." It's a real roaster, alright, and it features one of Jaco's finest recorded solos. His love of Latin music is amply on display here, along with his sharp sense of articulation.

Also note the rhythmic phrasing Jaco uses here that interacts with the rhythm section as an additional percussion instrument, even while soloing. It is important to maintain a sense of context during a solo, applying phrasing and note choices that reflect the musical context at hand. A steady stream of eighth notes in bebop style would be out of place in a Latin context. Throw yourself into the mix and play a solo that has meaning in the context of your musical surroundings.

(Used to Be A) Cha-Cha - Analysis

Measure #	Chord	Analysis
1–2	Dm9	Begins with 9th–11th–9th–♭3rd–5th–6th (D Dorian). Resolving to the 6th serves as a colorful modal device here.
3–4	Cm7	Jaco plays a bebop phrase that first outlines B♭maj7 and then, in measure 4, implies D minor.
5–6	A13♭9	Plays 3rd–♭9th. This is similar to the opening of the "Donna Lee" solo.
7–8	B♭7♯9	E♭ minor pentatonic sequence, highlighting a G♭ major triad in measure 7. This is an example of playing a triad a ♯5th from the root of an augmented 7th chord. He plays the 3rd, ♭9th, and ♯9th of the chord leading into the next change.
9–10	Cmaj7♭5	A descending arpeggiated figure outlines Cmaj7 and resolves to the 6th (A).
11–12	E♭7♯9–E♭6/9	In measure 11, the ♭5th–9th–root lick implies F7 over the E♭7 chord. This leads into a run that is basically a Cm9 arpeggio over the E♭ (the relative minor of the E♭6/9 chord). Notice the downward motion leading into the upward motion of the next phrase.
13–14	Dm7	Jaco plays a Bm7♭5 arpeggio in measure 13, which adds a major 7th (C♯) over the Dm7 chord. In measure 14, he plays the main bass line of the song, providing accompaniment to his own solo.
15–16	Cm7	Measures 15 and 16 outline Cm11 (3rd–11th–9th–7th–6th–5th–root). Here again, we see the upper extensions of the harmony moving to the root and 5th.
17–18	Dm7	This phrase is a sequential pattern of 4ths and minor 3rds based on the minor pentatonic scale, ending on B. Again, Jaco has resolved to the 6th on a minor 7th chord.
19–20	Cm7	In Jaco's own transcription, he has A7 written in parentheses. This indicates A7 superimposed over the harmony (Cm7), starting with an A altered scale figure. The second half of measure 20 begins his statement of the melody that continues for the next several measures.
21–22	Dm7	The carrying over of the A with the B♭ below implies B♭maj7 over the Dm7 harmony. The D minor figure in measure 22 resolves to the minor 3rd (F), which is the suspended 4th of the next chord.
23–24	Csus4	Here Jaco plays 3rd–2nd–6th (still quoting the melody).
25–26	A13♭9	Starts with 6th–♭9th and ends with 5th–4th–5th–6th. The 6th (F♯) of the A13 is also the ♯5th of the following B♭7♯9♯5 chord.
27–28	B♭7♯9♯5	After ending the quote of the melody with F♯, Jaco briefly walks up the A♭ minor scale, implies an F♯ major triad, and finally lands on an anticipation of the 6th (A♮) in the next chord.
29–30	Cmaj7♭5	Jaco plays 6th–3rd, followed by a brief C major walkdown into the next change.
31–32	E♭7♯9	Sequence of chromatically descending 6ths (5th–♭3rd and ♭5th–9th) resolves to root of chord.

(Used to Be A) Cha-Cha

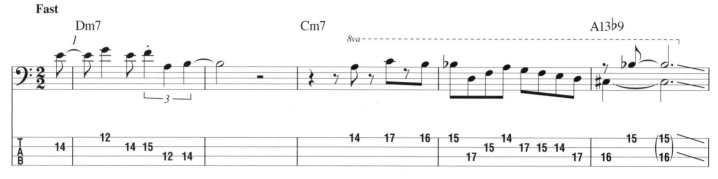

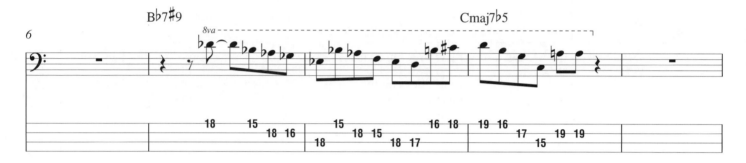

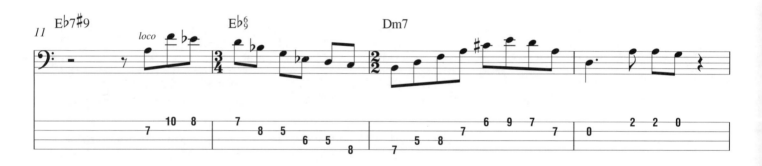

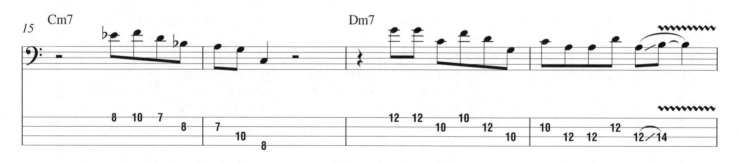

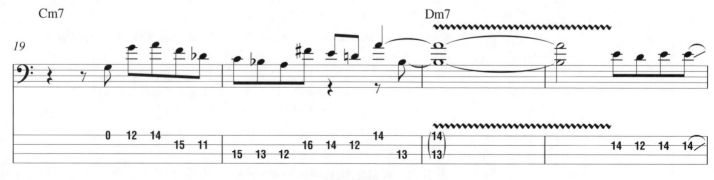

By Jaco Pastorius

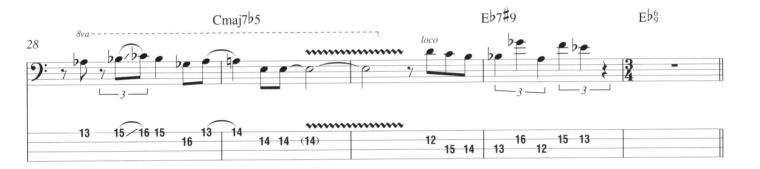

Teen Town

I remember calling Jaco one afternoon, after hearing he was off the road, to see if we could set up a lesson. He replied by asking me in his emphatic way, "What are you doing *right now*? I've got the new Weather Report album, and you have to hear this. When you hear this music, you don't hear drums, bass, or saxophone—you just hear music." I jumped into the car in eager anticipation. As usual, his grand statement turned out to be 100 percent correct. I still remember the excitement of hearing *Heavy Weather* for the first time. I had been a Weather Report fan since their first album, but the freshness of direction and vitality that Jaco brought to the band, and this album in particular, came leaping out of the speakers immediately. Contemporary classical, jazz, Latin, and R&B all meshed into one vibrant whole. Even though the album features amazing ensemble playing and virtuosic soloing, nothing disturbs the feeling of total organic unity. The clarity and depth of the production was astounding. I had the feeling I was witnessing the birth of a new type of music that disregarded labeling and stratification.

"Teen Town," the third cut from the album, features Jaco on drums as well as bass. The drums and bass carry on a dialog, answering each other throughout. Teen Town was a dance at a church in Pompano, Florida that Jaco used to go to as a youth. We can hear the marriage of bebop and modern classical with dance music (albeit rhythmically complex dance music—you won't hear drum fills like this in KC and the Sunshine Band). The influences of Jaco's early Florida days made themselves felt throughout his career.

On prominent display here is Jaco's sense of syncopation and, once again, phrasing. Every rhythm articulated here is part of the whole and has meaning in the overall texture of the tune. The drums and bass act as an extension of one another, each completing ideas started by its partner. Even though there are a lot of notes here, none are wasted. Note the extensive use of relative minor and simple (for Jaco, anyway) blues-type runs here. We get a feeling of juxtaposition of simple and complex, traditional and contemporary.

Teen Town - Analysis

Measure #	Chord	Analysis
1	C13	This sixteenth-note cross-string pattern outlines the C13 chord. The very last note of this measure anticipates the 3rd (C♯) of the next chord, A13.
2	A13	Descending root–6th–9th pattern, a classic example of Jaco resolving to a color tone (9th). This passage also outlines B7.
3	F13	The first half of this lick is a slightly syncopated version of a classic fifties R&B bass line. That's followed by a chromaticized F7 run up to the next chord.
4	D13	Jaco highlights the 6th and 9th in this lick before resolving to the root.
5	C13	Beginning with a chromatic lead-in note (D♯), Jaco features the 3rd and 5th of C13 and ends on the 9th again.
6	A13	A chromatic walkup to the 3rd, then a jump up to the root. Jaco then plays an F♯ (relative) minor pentatonic lick, ending on the 3rd of the chord.
7	F13	This 6th–5th–root motion answers the riff in measure 5.
8	D13	Syncopated chromatic walkup on D7, starting on the ♭7th.
9	C13	Jaco plays a bluesy A minor riff (relative minor of C). The notes are also the ♯9th, 9th, root, and 6th of the C13 chord.
10	A13	Chromatic A7 run starting on the root up to the 5th. He breaks the ascending pattern on the last three notes, playing the root, 7th, and ♭7th. The ♭7th of A13 is in anticipation of the 9th of the next chord.
11	F13	Plays ♭7th–6th–5th–6th–5th–root.
12	D13	Plays 5th–♭7th–root. The last two accented C notes (♭7th of D13) anticipate the root of the next chord.
13	C13	The 5th–6th–5th–root–9th–root sequence adds some pentatonic flavor to this measure.
14	A13	Jaco outlines F♯m7 and resolves to the 9th of A13. He ends the measure with a descending C minor pattern. The final C anticipates the 5th of the next chord, F13.
15	F13	Syncopated chromatic walkup from the root to the 9th.
16	D13	Jaco plays 4th–5th–♭7th. The C again anticipates the root of the next chord, C13 (start of the second chorus).

TRACK 52
fast demo
TRACK 53
slow demo

Teen Town

Moderately fast

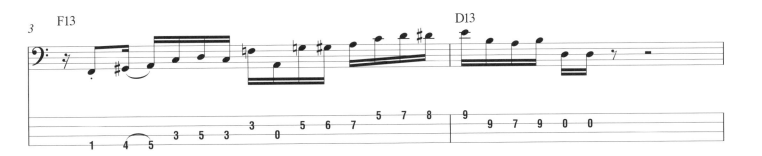

By Jaco Pastorius

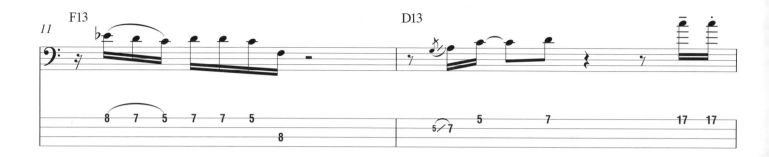

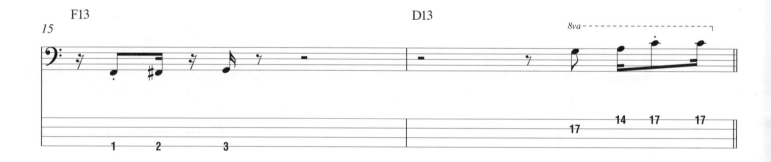

Havona

"The perfect and divine universe occupies the center of all creation; it is the eternal core around which the vast creations of time and space revolve. Paradise is the gigantic nuclear isle of absolute stability which rests motionless at the very heart of the magnificent eternal universe. This central planetary family is called Havona and is far distant from the local universe of Nebadon. It is of enormous dimensions and almost unbelievable mass and consists of one billion spheres of unimagined beauty and superb grandeur, but the true magnitude of this vast creation is really beyond the understanding grasp of the human mind."

—From *The Urantia Book*, Paper 14

This quote from *The Urantia Book*, a favorite of Jaco's, illustrates the source of inspiration for the ethereal piece of music that is "Havona," the closing number from *Heavy Weather*. Indeed, the feeling throughout suggests the "beauty and superb grandeur" of space. Rather than using harmony in a traditional, functional manner, Jaco splashes the chord voicings as if they were star clusters exploding light into space at regular intervals. Each chord stands as its own world, while remaining tied to the gravity of the universal whole. I often feel that his music has an other-worldly quality, married to the earthiest funk. The bass solo, in particular, alternates between wide intervallic spaciousness and blindingly-fast, dense passages, creating a wondrous musical thread of tension and release, expansion, and contraction. He starts inside, goes further out, and then brings it back home again in the usual brilliant Jaco fashion. Let's break down the first chorus.

Havona - Analysis

Measure #	Chord	Analysis
1–2	Emaj7♭5	The 5th–9th–3rd–5th motif gives a spatial sound to the solo opening.
3–4	Cmaj7	This root–♯4th–5th motif answers the one before it. F♯ gives the line a Lydian sound.
5–6	Bmaj7♭5	Jaco outlines the Bmaj7 chord and ends on the 6th (G♯). This line is a quote from the opening bassoon part of Stravinsky's *Rite of Spring*. He then walks up to the 5th and 6th to begin the next phrase.
7–8	Gmaj7	Playing the 9th–5th–6th, Jaco completes the thought from the opening while also answering the Stravinsky quote. The triplet figure in the next measure is a quote from the "Havona" melody.
9	Em9	The measure begins on the 9th, followed by an arpeggio outlining a Gmaj9 chord (relative major of Em). The last two notes of the arpeggio are then walked down in chromatic sequence to the next phrase. Rapid sixteenth notes contrast with the slower opening phrases.
10	Emaj7♭5	Begins with a sequence of major 3rds outlining Bmaj7 (7th–5th–♭5th–9th of Emaj7). He follows this with a 3rd–7th–6th figure that suggests the 6th–9th (G♯–C♯) of the Bmaj7 he just outlined.
11	Cmaj7	Jaco plays in A minor (relative minor of C) here, starting with an ascending minor scale up to the 5th, followed by 5–♭7–2–1 in A minor (which is also 3–5–7–6 in C).
12	Cmaj7	Here, Jaco begins a series of descending melodic sequences like the ones we covered in the "Melodic Elements" chapter. The first two outline D major (giving us the 13th–♯11th–9th extensions over Cmaj7) and C major triads respectively. He continues this pattern in the following measure.
13–14	Bmaj7♭5	Here, Jaco outlines C♯ and B major triads over Bmaj7♭5, continuing the pattern he began in the previous measure. He ends the phrase with a 7th–3rd–9th–7th–6th line that gives an open, pentatonic sound. Measure 14 ends with another statement of the C♯ major triad.
15–16	Gmaj7	After playing a B minor pentatonic figure to complete the thought started in measure 14, Jaco begins an extended burn on the B minor pentatonic scale. Measure 16 serves as a sort of "bridge" in descending motion to the lower register of the instrument.
17–21	Bm7	Jaco rips through some B minor pentatonic figures until the end of this chorus. Note the effective use of syncopation and his utilization of rests to increase tension in this section.

Havona

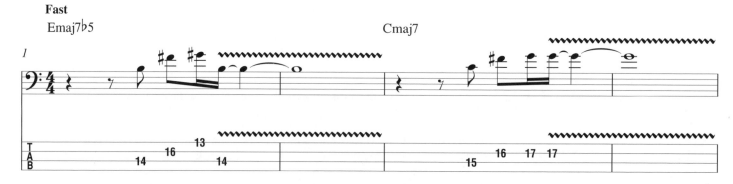

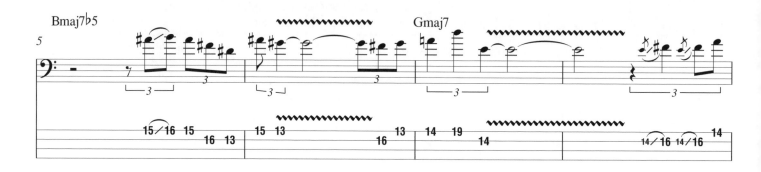

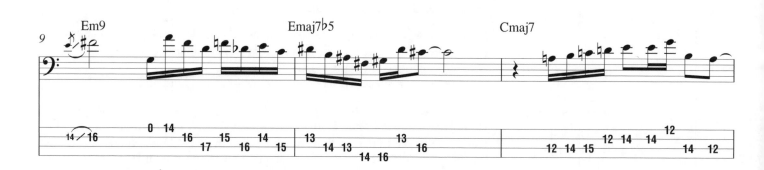

By Jaco Pastorius
Copyright © 1976 Haapala Music
Copyright Renewed
All Rights Reserved   Used by Permission

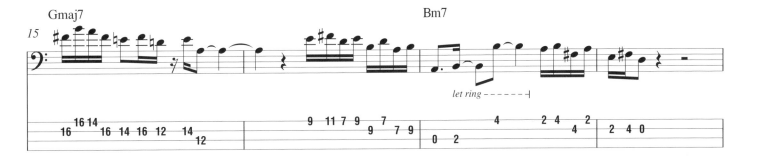

Chromatic Fantasy

My last lesson with Jaco took place on folding chairs in his backyard and centered on Bach's mighty "Chromatic Fantasy" from *Chromatic Fantasy and Fugue in D Minor*. I'll never be able to study or listen to Bach again without remembering one of Jaco's classic quotes from a few years earlier as we were looking at a Two-Part Invention:

"These cats talk about jazz. Man, Bach was Mr. Jazz!"

Having examined a lot of Bach's music, being both raised in the Lutheran church and studying classical music in college, I must confess that I never heard Bach that way. Nevertheless, as ever, Jaco was totally right on this count. A simple glance at measure 3 of "Chromatic Fantasy," for example, will readily prove Jaco's point. Compare this passage to the melody of the jazz standard, "Autumn Leaves." This measure spells out a cycle of Dm–Gm–C–F–B♭ (complete with a "blue note," C♯)–E°–A–Dm. This is a typical circle of fifths progression you will encounter time and again playing jazz standards.

As typical of Bach music, this piece contains measure after measure of chords spelled out melodically. For example, measure 1 is a progression from Dm–Em7♭5 (not played here)–Dm (first inversion)–Gm–A7♭9. This is repeated in a melodically inverted form for measure 2.

Your final assignment is to learn the "Chromatic Fantasy," taking note of the harmonic content of each measure. Rather than provide a complete analysis of the piece, I encourage you to analyze each passage for yourself, using the information you have gathered up to this point. This is the way Jaco taught me. He didn't spoon feed me all the information. Rather, he showed me the basic principles and guided me in analyzing the changes myself. Figuring out the harmony in this way will teach you to analyze what you hear and practice more effectively. This is a truly rewarding piece to play on the bass, so be diligent and patient as you master it. It is truly worth the effort.

Chromatic Fantasy

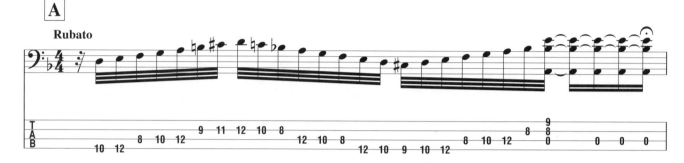

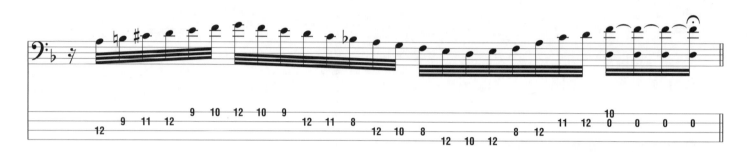

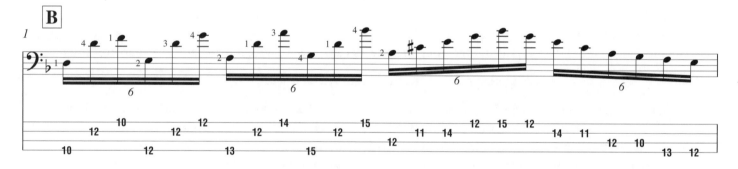

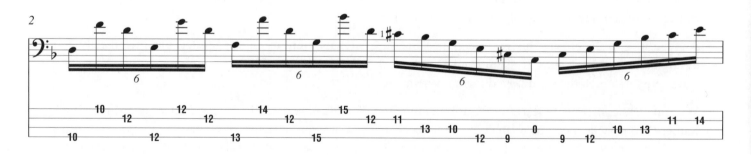

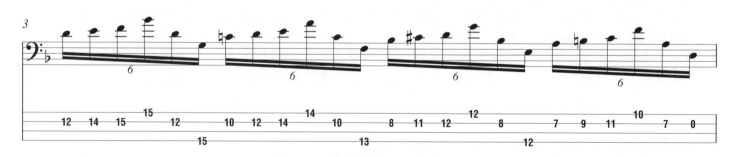

Arranged by Jaco Pastorius
Copyright © 1981 Mowgli Publishing
All Rights Reserved   Used by Permission

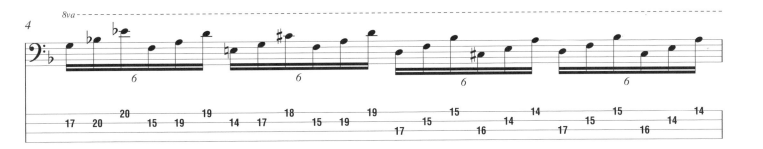

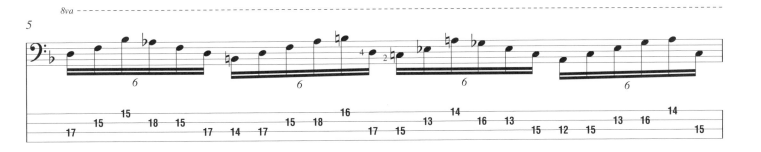

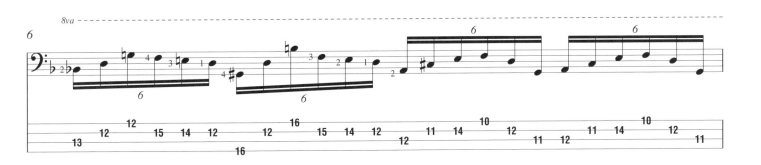

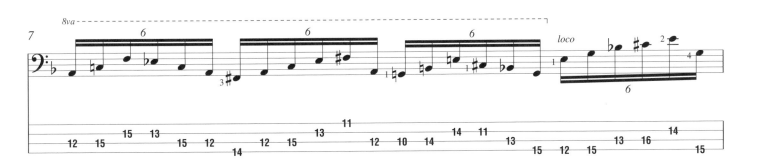

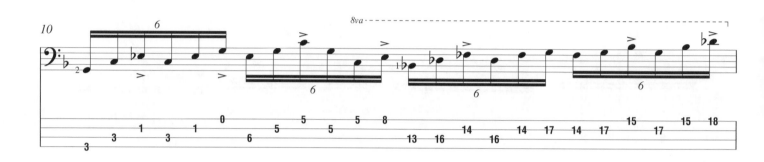

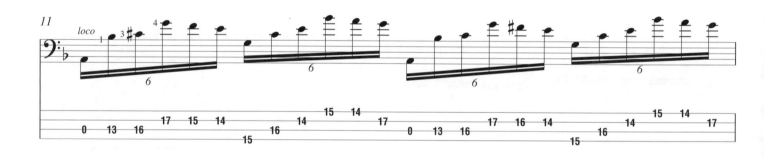

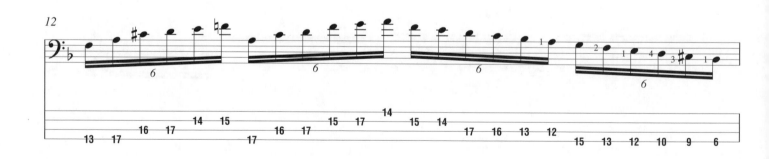

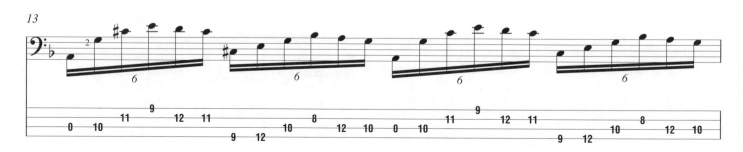

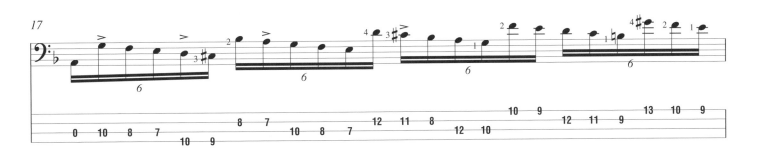

7. Food for Thought

Much of what has been written about Jaco posthumously centers around the troubled last period of his time on this Earth. A great deal of the commentary I've read portrays him as an unstable individual who happened to possess a freak musical genius, as if this talent was somehow disconnected from the man himself. Some well-meaning individuals who never met him suggest that we should remember him for his music, implying that we should overlook his personality. Such portrayals not only sell short the memory of a great man, they constitute historical inaccuracy. It is undeniable that there were poor chemical choices combined with emotional difficulties and self-destructive behavior in the last years. Certainly, Jaco was not the first great musician to explore these territories. This, unfortunately, gives birth to the kind of copy that sells newspapers and magazines. However, too few of the people who came in contact with him after his success in the music business (and none of those who never met him) really know about the great person behind the legend. I feel it is the responsibility of those of us who did know him to tell the other side of the story.

Jaco deserves equal fame for what he represented as a man. As I got to know him better, I came to realize that, as great as his passion for music was, he had his eyes on bigger accomplishments. I felt that he was looking to create a different type of human being (as well as a different world) in which art, intellect, philosophy, love of nature, and athletics all came together, much in the spirit of the ancient Greek philosophers. He absolutely loved to go to the beach with friends and family, to get out and revel in the glory of nature. Jaco loved to play baseball and basketball and did so with an absolutely fierce competitive spirit. He was also quite conscientious about being a good citizen of his country, extolling the virtues of filing an honest tax return and voting in elections. We had many philosophical discussions at our lessons as well, covering everything from religion to the pyramids to consciousness expansion. Jaco was a man of deep spiritual conviction. He saw music and life as inseparably connected and captured all of this brilliantly in his own work. I can visualize the Caribbean islands when I hear "Opus Pocus" or the Milky Way when I hear "Havona." Perhaps in a culture that gave greater support to its true artists, rather than deifying mere entertainers, Jaco could have gone much further in realizing these wider goals.

Another salient attribute of Jaco's character was his generosity of spirit toward other people. For all the much-discussed ego he brandished, I never knew him to put on a haughty air. Rather, he was always taking the time to talk to everyone who wanted to speak to him. He always seemed to have a genuine interest in other people's perspectives and a real love of humanity. If ever there were anyone who could, as Rudyard Kipling wrote, "...walk with kings, nor lose the common touch," that person would be Jaco Pastorius. He was always devoid of pretense or affectation. I was always amazed that, after months on the road with masters like Joe Zawinul and Herbie Hancock, he would still be interested in devoting time to furthering my own development. After about a year or so of studying with him, he surprised me one day at lesson's end by announcing that, inasmuch as he sensed my sincerity in wanting to become a better player, he would from that day no longer charge me for lessons. That's the kind of man he was.

Jaco was a tireless promoter of the value of positive thinking. He always encouraged me ("Mr. Snooze Alarm") to jump out of bed when the sun came up and say, "Yeah!" I recall a quote from one lesson regarding the importance of maintaining a confident mindset when playing. "It's, like, 75 percent mental attitude. If you're thinking to yourself, 'I'm happening,' then you're always swinging."

If I were to begin discussing Jaco's sense of humor, another entire volume might present itself. Suffice it say, there was rarely a shortage of laughter when he was around.

I urge you, the student, to focus on these attributes of Jaco as an artist and a man, leaving the "ritual sacrifice" aspect so prevalent in today's media to the mediocre and the gawkers. Jaco could not have achieved the musical greatness that he did without these character strengths. It is up to each of us as musicians to find those strengths within ourselves and project them in our own work.

Ultimately, I believe that Jaco accomplished the highest goal of our earthly existence on a very profound level. Namely, he affected those around him (and even countless people not around him) in such a way that their lives were forever enriched because of his presence. He freely shared his connection to the universal creative spirit with others.

Two decades after his passing, the strength of his work continues to provide this enrichment the world over, perhaps even more so than ever. Longevity is the real test of true art, and Jaco continues to pass that test with flying colors. In a business long dominated by mediocrity and the glorification of all that is base, Jaco's work still shines like an absolute lighthouse. His dominance on the bass guitar remains unassailable. To this day, no young artist has come along to rock the jazz world like Jaco did, despite a succession of gifted players. Yet, for all his magnificent artistic accomplishments, I will always remember the guy who basked in the Florida sun as readily as the spotlight, loved his family dearly, lived each moment to the fullest, always gave freely of his time to guide people (like myself) musically and personally, and refused to be intimidated by either the often absurd realities of the music business or the opinions of the naysayers. I will always equate Jaco with the ideals of independence and of fearlessly forging one's own destiny, despite any and all odds. He was a true renaissance man, a pioneer, and a powerful creative spirit. From the bottom of my heart, I thank you, Mr. Pastorius, for your guidance and friendship over the years. Whatever music you're writing over on the other side, I'm sure it will amaze us all.

Ray Peterson
February, 2008

Acknowledgments

Thanks to the Pastorius family.

Many kind thanks to Jeff Schroedl, Eric Wills, and Kurt Plahna at Hal Leonard.

Special thanks to Bob Bobbing for setting things up and kindly allowing me access to the Library. I couldn't have done it without you.

Last but not least, effusive thanks to John Francis Anthony Pastorius III.

About the Author

Ray Peterson grew up in Fort Lauderdale, FL. After playing in numerous rock bands, he started his professional career playing R&B in Miami with such groups as Jesse James & the Outlaws, Tommy Strand and the Upper Hand, and many others. Ray studied double bass with Frank Carroll, playing with the Broward Symphony Orchestra. He subsequently began private studies with Jaco Pastorius, later playing with Florida jazz greats like steel drummer Othello Molineaux and saxophonist Ben Champion, in addition to standards gigs and shows such as Robert Goulet, Al Martino, Eddie Fisher, and others. In 1987, Ray relocated to New York, where he quickly landed the bass spot with the legendary saxophonist Eddie Harris. He has also performed with Les McCann, Blood Sweat and Tears, Shalom Hanoch, Paul Butterfield, Mike and Leni Stern, and The Funky Tenor All-Stars, featuring Eddie Harris, Pee Wee Ellis, Karl Denson, and Larry Goldings. He has also recorded a CD of original material entitled *Galaxy Club*. He has recently been performing with his brother, blues-rock guitarist Ronnie Peterson. Ray is currently working on multiple projects. You can find more information at myspace.com/raypetersonbass.